ST UBS

A Father's Tickets to the Greatest Shows on Earth

Michael Wellman

Outskirts Press, Inc.
Denver, Colorado

For Duke & Derber [Bill & Tom]

Outta here, but safe at home…

STUBS
A Father's Tickets to the Greatest Shows on Earth
All Rights Reserved.
Copyright © 2011 Michael Wellman
v3.0

Outskirts Press, Inc.
http://www.outskirtspress.com

ISBN: 978-1-4327-6416-6

Outskirts Press and the "OP" logo are trademarks belonging to Outskirts Press, Inc.

PRINTED IN THE UNITED STATES OF AMERICA

ACKNOWLEDGMENTS

Before this goes any further I want to credit Joey Early for the cover design and photography. He gave me what I envisioned. I hope the stuffing measures up to his contribution.

Other than that I think I better just give thanks.

MW

"The camera makes everyone a tourist in other people's reality, and eventually in one's own."
~ Susan Sontag; author & political activist ~

"There have been only two authentic geniuses in the world - Willie Mays and Willie Shakespeare. But, darling, I think you'd better put Shakespeare first."
~ Tallulah Bankhead; bon vivant extraordinaire ~

PREFACE

A long time ago and with no intention of this I started saving tickets from events I attended, whether alone or with all or part of our family.

At the end of a day when I'd empty my pockets onto the dresser, if there were ticket stubs, I usually kept them. The practice was partly a result of my uncertainty as to what's garbage and what's treasure; the same dynamic that's responsible for the emergence of the garage/porch/yard sale as the Great American Bazaar. But it was also my way of preserving and later jogging memories.

I began stashing used tickets in an old wooden desktop box my wife gave me as a Christmas present one year, she having picked up on my penchant for keepsakes and mementos.

At some point I became annoyed by the increasingly ubiquitous cameras of all sorts that mar and distort the way we live, work and play with one another now. Even the most ordinary among us is attended on occasion by at least one personal paparazzo, and for what - a chance at going viral on the internet? Some poorly framed, badly lit pics of just another day in the life of who - you? We have become a nation of hams and bad actors, contriving every scene that we might star in it.

I don't have bad memories of good times. But films and photos, for all their pixels, sometimes fail us. The difference between them and the mind's eye can be the difference between the unexpected sighting of an animal in the wild and a ho-hum stroll past one asleep in the zoo.

If it is more or less true that a picture is worth a thousand words, then what follows here could more easily have been accomplished by several dozen snapshots. Alas, I don't often carry a camera, though we do keep one at home just in case.

Some time ago, when I was rummaging through the box I discovered there was at least a scrapbook in there, maybe more.

First Comes Love

It was a Saturday in November of 1990 - football weather - when my wife told me that the last pass I'd made at her was complete. She - we - was pregnant. Touchdown!

Some 15 months after we huddled up in wedlock and just a few since we'd decided to expand the roster and make the bold move from couple to family, we were on the board.

It can be a vain and inexact enterprise, this mixing of gene pools in hopes of literally making some love. You can't measure out a pinch of curly hair and a dash of blue eyes without the risk of accidentally spilling in some allergies and bad toenails. You might concoct a girl as pretty as her mother who's as much a gasbag as her dad. But we nevertheless poured ourselves into one another, mostly blind to the possible chemical and biological permutations. Blind too was the portion of faith that was in the mix.

For the luckiest of our species the launch into existence is a culmination of deliberate planning. To be conceived first in the hearts and minds, and only then in the baser machinery of one's folks is a generally better thing than birthing onto the scene of an accident; one that unfolds across lifetimes after the frenzied first in the chain of events that begins it.

If life is to be much of a party it helps to arrive by invitation.

And so Max did the following summer, at which point a lot of well-laid plans began to go awry.

We knew our first-born was going to be a stand-up person, shall we say, since an ultrasound early on revealed the telltale sign. We'd intended to be surprised by gender in the delivery room, but there was no keeping this secret from us once we knew it was there for the taking.

Armed with this key bit of information we bandied prospective names back and forth throughout the last two trimesters. Max was nowhere on the list. Cole was. So was Nick. They were the two finalists when we met our son face-to-face for the first time.

Suddenly Max barged into the discussion. Chris' paternal grandfather was named Max [Middleton]. She'd been close to her grandparents, especially so as a young girl, and the death of her grandma, Max's wife Mary, about a month before our wedding had tempered the nuptial festival a little.

So Chris lobbied hard for Max. I liked the simplicity of it and its potential for nicknaming. But really, the overriding factor was the wrongness of saying no to a woman just after a whole brand new person has tortuously eked from inside her. Corporations pay less for the naming rights to magnificent edifices. Max it was. We slapped on a subtitle of Jacob from my branch of the tree to complete the monogram and took the kid home to start familying.

I started calling him Jackpot. Whenever I was on duty and he indicated that it was time for a fresh pair of trousers, I'd open the used ones and exclaim, "JACKPOT!" He'd grin a knowing grin that said, "I've gotcha pal, and there's nothing you can do about it." It's the "sign here" grin; you've got yerself a lifetime deal.

These ceremonial changings-of-the-pants and the wettings-of-the-whistle that led to them were my first father & son collaborations with me in the lead role. They were rudimentary but mutually satisfying, enough so that I eagerly explored Chris to see who else she was hiding in there.

In due course Max was joined in our brood by Ben and Emma.

Ben was born on Babe Ruth's birthday, February 6, in 1994; our very own "Bambino!" He got off to something of a false start in a couple of ways. So breathless was he upon arrival that he spent a couple of weeks at the hospital getting the wind knocked into him. In those first days his nametag read "Jonathan Michael." Our first choice was always Benjamin, but we had an already over-bearing neighbor named Ben. Afraid that he would mistakenly see our second-born as his namesake and an invitation to pester us even more, we opted initially for Plan J. When news broke just after the birth that neighbor Ben and his wife were moving west to retire in Arizona we got out the eraser and drove home the only BMW we're likely ever to afford.

Emma completed our hat trick in December, 1996. Her birthday on the 19th has ever since served as the kickoff in our house to Christmas Week. Her name was plucked from the marquee at *The Varsity*, the long-standing, free-standing movie house of my youth hard by the campus of Drake University that's seen me all the way from Tarzan to Jane Austen. The name struck us then as old-fashioned and uncommon without sounding as though we were trying to invent a tag as unique as our little snowflake. Now

3

it's overused.

Like Ben, his little sister lingered at the hospital for a time collecting herself before making a grand entrance and debut at home on New Year's Eve.

Glad to have drawn a girl instead of a third jack, Chris and I wisely quit while way ahead. We were three for four, having suffered the setback of a miscarriage between Max and Ben; a question mark that interrupted a series of exclamation points. Even there, something was created that still persists.

My faucet of progeny was shut off not long after Emma flowed from it. The procedure that saw to this seemed too perfunctory and routine given its serious purpose, not to mention painless. I lay there with my hands clasped behind my head, chatting casually with the doctor while he blockaded the narrow canal that had been my passage to the wide ocean of immortality.

I reveled in the making of our family, each stage of it. I cheered each announcement of pregnancy like a gawker at a blastoff. I lay happily awake at night throughout gestations contemplating the swelling belly next to me as though it were a crystal ball. I thought my wife looked especially beautiful when she was carrying us around inside of her.

Whole new sections and departments of stores and malls drew my interest. I formed opinions and preferences arbitrarily about a wide range of products; everything from disposable diapers to car seats and strollers. I began to see myself as the great provider of goods and services, a stallion who would facilitate the remarkability of prodigies, first genetically and then in untold other ways.

I'm not sure precisely when the panic first set in, but I can look back now and recognize glimmers of it in pictures of me holding Max within minutes of his birth. There is a singular cast to my face, the new color that results from the blending of pure awe and abject fear. Am I holding a treasure or a squirming vessel of nitroglycerin that I dare not drop lest my world be blown to smithereens?

Watching a new father at work is to observe a fascinating phenomenon. Whereas most women are magnetized to infants in general, men typically avoid them as they would a jewelry store. Yes, they're precious, but also fragile and expensive and you can't really do anything with them. But then you get one of your own. Music isn't the only way to soothe the savage beast. It's quite a thrill the first time your child falls peacefully asleep in your arms. Instead of the "gotcha pal" grin that accompanied the unveiling of the diaper pies, Max, Ben and Emma; each in their turn, fixed me with an "I trust you, dad" gaze on their way to sleep in my care that was deeply reassuring.

That look is not unlike the one dogs are capable of that makes you feel all-powerful. They seem convinced that you are the source of all things and it is only our own children and dogs that can make us feel god-like. Their occasional disobedience pales in the shade of their lovability and they are also good trainers under the guise of being trainees.

It was beside the point that the kids' options were limited in those days and they were behooved to inspire some paternal self-confidence if they hoped to survive infancy. Later, of course, after their optic muscles had developed sufficiently and they'd gotten their feet under them, they all advanced to exaggerated eye rolling in response to most of my behaviors, but by then we were hopelessly stuck with each other.

Once secure in the realization that I posed no real, immediate threat to the safety of my children, I began to think that the early stages of child development might not actually be so treacherous, at least not for me as the father. After all, the basic training consisted mostly of stuff I'd mastered: rolling over, crawling, walking, talking and eating with the hands were all things I was certified in and glad to demonstrate as many times as it took. Role modeling couldn't have been more elementary. Granted, taking someone along as an observer to the more refined method of defecation was at first inhibiting for the demonstrator and perhaps disenchanting for the apprentice, but still, steady progress was made by both father and child[ren].

Early on in a child's life people scrutinize and probe in search of resemblances. Parents thrill at the bequeathal of their eye and hair color to the next generation, but then the less flattering traits, the ones evolution hasn't had time for yet, start to emerge. "Oh look! He's got his daddy's impatience, obsessiveness and assorted other neuroses! Isn't that cute?"

It was as though the magician's fingers had snapped, awakening me from the trance whereby I'd been convinced that someone inherently and irrevocably like me might also be somehow wholly different and special. Do you think of yourself as someone special? Most of us would like to be, but strongly suspect that we are not. We realize at some point that we are unique only in ways that work to our detriment and make life impossibly difficult.

For me, that honeymoon phase of fatherhood when I was thrilled that our beautiful kids might be chips off the old block inevitably yielded to the much longer, indefinite and ongoing stage where I worry that our beautiful kids might be chips off the old block. That small, preferred mirror, mirror on the wall at home that makes you look your best gives way to the full-length, brightly lit, all-dimensional one that tells you the harder truths about yourself.

Never possessed of the requisite hand-eye coordination for juggling say, three apples, I began to suspect that neither could I manage to juggle three kids. The preliminaries are misleadingly paced; sort of like the way a roller coaster ride begins by slowly easing away from the loading gate. Babies move slowly; their territory is flat and limited. But next thing you know one of them is riding a bike out of the driveway into the street while another is wobbling out the back door with an eye-putter-outer, the third is crawling across the floor toward a sleeping dog with a playfully ignorant expression, and you're doing the parental algebra in your head and coming up with an equation that results in mayhem no matter how you work it.

Of course the prototype bears the brunt of the novice father's trials and errors.

Once as I bent over Max's changing table I rose up too abruptly and my head dislodged a small shelf mounted on the wall. Curios rained down around us. Max was startled but otherwise unscathed. The objects bounced off of me and did not touch him, setting a false precedent for the rest of his life.

Another time as I was shooing him in from the front porch I pinched his hand in the hinge of the door. Somewhere deep in the subconscious layers of him that event must be stored as a turning point. The acute pain of that moment gave way to the permanent and mutual realization that not only was I incapable of shielding him from all things at all times, I might even occasionally be an inadvertent inflictor.

Luckily for all concerned there was the mother.

There was no paternal gaffe that she couldn't undo; no deed done dadly she couldn't put right.

I was permitted to chaperone the livestock in the same spirit that the kid who brings the bat gets to play in the game even though he's no good. Then too, Chris did have to rest occasionally, despite that her sleep requirement declined in inverse proportion to the heightened sensual acuity that she has displayed ever since becoming a mother, on a scale in the range of super-powers. She began to hear ants making their way across our driveway as though they were a herd of cattle stampeding toward her child's crib. A stalk of celery removed from the fridge three rooms away…sniff, sniff - smells like trouble; where are the kids?

She has not slept a whole night through since sometime prior to July 9, 1991, the date when she went into labor with Max.

Mothers are the ones who bake the cakes. They have the eggs but need a stick of butter, so they come knocking on the door of their neighbor, the man. They mix everything, they bake it, they deliver it fresh from their oven; it's theirs. Butterman doesn't generally like cake much, but since he contributed to this one and does like bakers, he thinks it's delicious.

You figure you've got about five years to have your cakes and eat 'em too. By then the outside world is clamoring at your door for a piece of 'em.

Max couldn't wait. He used to stand in the front yard on our side of the, yes, picket fence, and wave and cheerfully holler hello to passersby. Not a few of them either ignored him or reacted as if they'd been accosted. It was a role reversal; adults wary of the friendly little stranger on Harwood Drive. What was he up to? What's wrong with his parents?

We sent him off to school with the same mixed feelings of 4H kids who raise a lamb for the county fair; anxious for the officials to see our blue ribbon project but sad because we knew he'd soon be getting sheared.

A few days in he went to bed one night, still in character as the happily adjusting kindergartner. Chris and I sat smugly rejoicing in the living room, toasting each other with projections of Max's future like sips from a fine genetic potion we'd brewed.

Suddenly our reverie was interrupted when Max reappeared. He had a confession to deliver. He was miserable and wanted to quit school. "This just isn't working out," was how he put it - from wunderkind to dropout in less than a week.

The honeymoon was over and our three ring circus was about to begin. It was time for some tougher love than we'd been serving up so far. By this time Ben was toddling about, banging into and bouncing off of things, and Chris was pregnant with Emma. We had no choice but to force Max back into the fray of half-day kindergarten. He found a good friend and together they managed. Max named him and David "the soft guys" and they pulled each other through the strange new land of bullies and bad language. During Christmas break Emma was born. Now Max had a little sister to blaze a trail for. He embraced the added burden. By year's end he was hardened and ready for the challenge of all-day school. Bring on 1st grade!

Happily the broadening horizons of life extended beyond the schoolyard. If we were compelled to send Max out alone each day as a scout for his brother and sister, there were also more occasions by then for wider-ranging outings together.

Always a sports fan, born in the rookie year of Ernie Banks and Henry Aaron, I'd been anxious for some time to go to ballgames with my own kids so I could impart my athletic wisdom and reveal the subtleties of games, especially baseball, that were lost on most folks, even the majority of those others who attended them. Naturally we'd made some preliminary visits to local ballparks when there was no hope of real understanding, just an exercise in the wasting of money. Hot dogs too big to eat; cotton candy too big to see around and soft drinks too big to grip. And of course the squirts had to be properly outfitted. Nothing breaks in a new baseball glove quite like a rub comprised of mustard, peanut shells and soda pop, certified with the indecipherable autograph of an anonymous minor leaguer. Pound your fist in the pocket of that sucker now!

I paid scant heed when Max stood nose to screen, transfixed during Diana Ross' performance at the 1996 Super Bowl halftime show and declared, "someday I'm gonna do that." As a matter of fact, let me confess in a spirit of full disclosure that I would've forgotten his offhanded remark had my wife not captured it on our obligatory camcorder. Anyhow…

If Max seemed about ready [I know I was] for discussions of the finer points of baseball as the spring of the year when he would later start kindergarten loomed, I had no illusions as to his readiness for actually playing the game in any recognizable fashion at that stage. So I was surprised to learn when Max was four that the next year he would be eligible to sign up for something called "tee-ball" at Raccoon Valley, the same little league where I'd played decades earlier at a time when you had to be at least nine years old to join.

Tee-ball is no closer a relative of baseball than Cro-Magnon was of Jerry Falwell.

The outer diamond at the periphery of the little league complex where the tee-ballers and their handlers were exiled for the early Saturday morning dew-sweepers was more or less directly beneath the take-off and landing patterns of nearby Des Moines International. Sort of like Shea Stadium and LaGuardia in New York. No surprise then that signal fires sometimes flared up in the outfield. Once some kids laid down in an S-O-S formation! But even then they were too small to be seen by low-flying aircraft. There was no escaping tee-ball.

If Max was to ever enjoy baseball drastic action was called for before he was banished to the outskirts of Raccoon Valley.

Opening Day

Was it by divine intervention that there was a cut-rate airline serving Des Moines in the spring of 1996 offering $50 round trip fares to Chicago? I had by then made many a sojourn to Wrigley Field, but never with my own offspring and never for Opening Day.

Opening Day is my personal New Year's Day, coming as it does on the wings of spring and songbirds instead of in the bleak and bare-treed mid-winter. No matter that the launching of each new season prefaces the funeral pyre that awaits Cub fans somewhere short of the Holy Grail that is the World Series. In the springtime the season itself is more than enough, regardless of where it shall go and how it's likely to resolve.

Ordinarily I don't make my first pilgrimage of the year too soon. For all her splendor on a sunny day in July, Wrigley without her ivy on a cold day in April can be a shrew. It's usually around Memorial Day before temperatures are warm enough to waken the dormant vines that soften the unforgiving brick walls each summer and turn them an irresistible shade of real, live green.

But this was an emergency. My first-born son's future was at stake. I bought two plane tickets and two tickets to the Cubs' season opener. Their opponent was to be the San Diego Padres. If you ask me why the game wasn't scheduled in balmy San Diego instead of frosty Chicago I'd chalk it up to the fact that the appointed date was April Fools' Day.

There were nearly 40,000 other fools waiting for us by the time Max and I arrived at the ballpark. We were dressed the same way we would have been if we'd been going tobogganing. The temperature was in the high 30's. We'd gotten up that morning at dawn to be sure we got to the airport in plenty of time for the 350 mile, 45 minute flight from Des Moines to Chicago.

From O'Hare we made our way to the ballpark on the "L." It actually took us longer to get from the airport to the ballpark than it had to get from Des Moines to Chicago. We had to transfer once and at some point I hoisted Max on my shoulders as we hiked through an underground tunnel from one train to the next. I started to wonder if I'd assigned the kid too big a day. After all, I was in my early 40's and an incurable Cub fan who'd never been to Opening Day. Max wasn't really presenting with symptoms yet, though I was trying hard to infect him. He hadn't seen Wrigley at her resplendent best and now was going to get his first up close look at her before she had a chance to put on her makeup. He sometimes talked in those days of becoming an Expo fan based on his attraction to their logo.

The Montreal Expos were a team even more ill-fated than the Cubs, soon to succumb to the financial asphyxia of fan indifference, a team so star-crossed that the one year, 1994, when they appeared to be the best and bound for the World Series, the event was cancelled on account of labor strife.

The Cubs, by comparison, are simply afflicted with a chronic case of mediocrity from which they can neither recover nor suffer by any criterion other than the league standings; the worst thing, really, any team can be - complacent also-rans. And yet they have become over the course of a century or so of shortfall one of our culture's most popular lost causes.

It hasn't always been thus. There used to be a perverse elitism that accrued to Cub loyalists. From my own boyhood until not all that long ago Cub tickets were easily afforded and obtained by those so inclined. Until the late 20th century the team performed for less than capacity audiences most of the time and those who did take themselves out to the ballgame brought along low expectations. I saw very few games in person as a kid and the only one I ever went to with my father didn't happen until I was grown and he was nearing the end of his career as a lifelong fan of the team. Mostly we commiserated together via radio broadcasts and box scores in the morning sports page.

Family history is a reliable predictor of many ailments. So it was that my father afflicted me with the pain in the ass and pang in the heart that are the Cubs, and so would it be with me and mine, by god! But was I making too bold a move too soon? Would this grand excursion backfire and disenchant the boy just as I feared tee-ball might a year henceforth?

The Cubs fell in arrears by a count of 2-0 in the early innings. The frigid temperature was somewhat negated by the sun that hung like a prop if nothing more over the diamond-shaped stage and outdoor auditorium we were squeezed into. It was a day that cried out for refreshments like hot chocolate and coffee but an army of beer vendors nevertheless patrolled the ballpark emptying their trays and filling their pockets. Never a full minute passed without one from their ranks passing through and pausing to block our view while doing some business in our section. It seemed like nobody was watching either the game or their language.

I was just a couple years sober at the time and so got irritated by the vendors, their patrons and the score. Actually, it was progress that I wasn't tempted by the beermen. When I finally confronted the reality of my alcoholism I was afraid that my apparent fondness for ballgames and ballparks would be exposed as nothing more than a ruse that facilitated pathological drinking. It was a relief to rediscover that I did indeed enjoy the just-right mix of methodical strategy, bursts of physical prowess and livin'-is-easy weather that are baseball at its best.

But beer has long outsold peanuts and crackerjack combined and continues to without my contribution, so I guess it served me right to take this peek in that mirror I mentioned a while back.

Max got into a four year-old's spirit of the occasion and declared that he'd like some ice cream, none of which was for sale in the stands. We went below into the bowels beneath the grandstand to relieve ourselves, standing abreast of one another, man to man, trying to get enough extension to squirt into the urinal troughs without dampening our parkas before setting out to find a concession stand offering frosty malts and the like.

Finally we spied a booth lit up with colorful depictions of ice cream cones and fudgesicles. We approached and placed an order. The dispenser on duty fixed us with the same stare he might have reserved for Martians.

"We're not selling ice cream today!" he sneered, as if bothered by a couple of scavenger hunters. "It's too cold - how 'bout some nachos?"

We got back to our seats in time to see the Cubs' short shortstop, Rey Sanchez, hit a two-run homer that tied the game. It was the only one he would swat all season.

The Cubs later took the lead on another two-run homer, this one by Scott Servais, a journeyman catcher, only to have the Padres tie the game in the top of the 9th, a perfect here-we- go-again moment to launch the long campaign.

But the Cubs won the game dramatically in the bottom of the 10th when Mark Grace singled in the winning run. Gloved and mittened hands both muffled and prolonged the crowd's ovation. We lingered, waiting for the clogs at the exits to clear and savoring that the Cubs were undefeated frontrunners out of the gate. By the time we finally straggled out the place was like an electric appliance that had been unplugged. 40,000 watts drained outside and headed home.

We retraced our route to the airport, at first packed claustrophobically onto the "L" but gradually we took space vacated by passengers who left at stops somewhere between Addison Street and O'Hare Airport. By the time we needed to disembark and switch from train to plane, Max was unfurled across two seats, barely awake.

I roused him and the bustle of the terminal brought him alert. We had a short wait to endure once we reached our gate which we passed with more snacks on top of the ballpark fare that had sustained us all afternoon. By the time our flight was called a metropolitan commuter pace that neither of us was accustomed to had begun taking its toll, particularly on Max, whose general awe at the twin spectacle of his first plane flight and first big league ballgame rolled into the same day was being overtaken by sheer exhaustion. But he rallied one more time when the pilot of our flight home invited him into the cockpit as we boarded, gave him a clip-on pair of wings and slapped the captain's hat on him.

We landed safely back in Des Moines, found our car in the parking garage and drove the last 15 minutes of our incredible journey. By the time we pulled into the driveway the sun was gone and so was Max. I carried him inside and put him in bed. Then I was debriefed by his mother.

It would be several years before Max told us that he had undertaken that adventure expecting that when our plane from Des Moines neared Chicago we would be issued parachutes and told when to jump out. And that when we boarded for the trip back he thought he was being invited to fly the jet.

I guess he was willing to take a shot at both.

Free Opening Day caps were passed out at the Wrigley Field turnstiles that day. The year isn't specified and that's appropriate since the occasion is a timeless rite. I think we both got one but I can only find one of them now. It's still a bright royal blue but closet storage has rumpled it to the point that it doesn't conform very well to the head anymore, if it ever did. It's a cheap bauble that nevertheless unlocks a trunk full of sentiment, reflection and memory.

Max and I had journeyed to the big leagues and lived to tell about it. We have returned many times in the years since, and the itineraries have varied enough to remind me of NASA's manned space programs from my boyhood. The durations of our time in orbit expanded. We added crew members. We traveled greater distances. Someday we will walk on the moon of the World Series.

What's the Word?
Fight, Fight, @#%*!

Max's apprenticeship as a sports fan took its next big step later that same year when I snagged a couple of tickets to the Iowa Hawkeyes' first football game of the season. The date was September 7, 1996, the opponent was the University of Arizona and the venue was Kinnick Stadium in Iowa City.

Given that the football schedule would run the seasonal gamut of weather from summery to wintry conditions, it was appropriate that the Hawks were slated to begin against a team from the desert and finish just before Thanksgiving versus their traditional rivals from the tundra to the north, the Minnesota Gophers.

STUBS

Whereas we'd been outfitted like Eskimos for our baseball adventure in April, now we set out for a first taste of big-time college football clad lightly in shorts and t-shirts. Such is the overlap of the ever-lengthening athletic seasons anymore that the old handbooks for appropriate fan attire are obsolete. In the sporting world one may acceptably dress oneself in white, or team-colored body paint for that matter, before Memorial Day, after Labor Day, or whenever.

Chris packed us a cooler full of sandwiches, cookies and sodas and we shared an early breakfast at home before loading into the car for the 100 mile drive to my alma mater.

I graduated from Iowa in 1976. The football team was hapless while I was there, plummeting to the nadir of an 0-11 season in 1973. The student section was the site of many a toast of resignation. It was in these ranks that I became accustomed to a more potent class of elixirs ranging from schnapps to Jack Daniels to an especially virulent Mogen David vintage that was labeled 20/20, not because it sharpened one's eyesight - it was more likely to induce temporary blindness - but as a marketer's boast as to its proof and potency. Everyone called it Mad Dog; a transient yet collegiate nectar best aged in brown bags with a not so subtle bark at the palate that flowed into an absolutely savage bite upon absorption into the circulatory system - especially good with stadium fare, swigged right from the bottle!

This inaugural tailgate experience with Max was hardly reminiscent of my campus days. We parked a mile or so west of the stadium in a big grassy lot across from Finkbine, the university golf course. After fortifying ourselves with the pre-game ration of our provisions we tossed a small football back and forth to get ourselves in the proper mood. As had been the case some five months earlier at Wrigley Field, we were surrounded by others whose warm-ups were, shall we say, more fluid than our own.

I suppose that I was more or less in the throes of a rampant paternal syndrome that causes a man to vividly imagine his heir growing into a veritable Achilles, if only the man ensures to properly guide him and supplement what's already been passed through the loins with wisdom gained on gridirons, diamonds and courts of hard experience. I don't actually remember feeling that way, but I surely must have; the condition is nearly as common as male births.

There springs this irrepressible hope that you've sired a thorough-bred; a champion; and that if somehow you truly have, that truth shall be revealed for all the world to know in the athletic arena, for how else could anybody tell? It starts as soon as you report for your infants' regular checkups at the doctor. 90 days out of the womb and the kid is off the growth charts! Yes [fist pump]! He wobbles to his feet after a year or so and staggers across the living room like a sailor on a weekend pass and you see a sprinter breaking the tape in the Olympic 100 meter dash.

On this particular occasion I was probably on the lookout for pre-cursors of a latent machismo, some kindergartenized manifesta-tion of a penchant for collision that would later facilitate the mak-ing of a football player.

Instead what I had, what we always had with Max, was a happy, friendly kid.

I chafed at the too-narrow seats in the stadium. The distance between the numerals painted on the minimalist benches where all sizes and shapes of asses were supposed to perch was barely enough for even one average sized buttock, let alone a pair. The still-warm weather of early September allowed for lighter clothing but also made for sweaty, sometimes smelly bench mates. A throng bundled against November might not be quite so scented, but how would it fit?

Ten years later a renovation of Kinnick Stadium was undertaken which included the widening of each bench seat for the rank and file fans to the tune of two additional inches! This equates roughly to giving a poor man two cents, but does at least allow one rooter to dislodge their arm from another's armpit and thrust it skyward, whether to signal an Iowa touchdown or protest an injustice levied against the home team by the referees. In that case a middle finger often juts from the fully extended arm[s] like the radio tower atop the Empire State Building and broadcasts the low brow signal of a partisan clad in old gold and black.

A more significant feature of the project was the erection of a statue of Nile Kinnick, he from whom the place takes its name, outside a new main entrance plaza at the south end of the premises.

Kinnick grew up in Adel, Iowa and remains the lone Iowa player to win the annually awarded Heisman Trophy, emblematic of the nation's outstanding college football player. Kinnick earned the honor as the star of Iowa's 1939 "Ironmen" squad. His speech in acceptance of his prize at the New York Athletic Club is generally regarded as the finest one yet offered by any recipient.

Kinnick personified most of the attributes anyone would want in their child or any country would want in a native son. He was bright, handsome, articulate, patriotic, unselfish and, oh yes, athletic. Remarkably, he hailed from the same neck of America's woods as Hall-of-Fame pitcher Bob Feller; even catching him for a time on an area baseball team when they both were schoolboys.

That Kinnick died in military service as a young soldier on a training flight in the Pacific during WWII was the greatest of tragedies at the time [he was the first Heisman Trophy winner to die] but is also what finally cast him in the bronze monument where he now stands in Iowa City. Significantly, he is depicted with a letter jacket slung over his shoulder and a stack of schoolbooks under his free arm. The NCAA, governing body of big-time college sports, likes to use the term student-athlete in reference to kids on athletic scholarship. Those to whom it legitimately applies could as well be called Nile Kinnicks.

If the statue had been there on this day in 1996 I would have posed my small son near it and snapped his picture. These days you take your shots with genuine sports heroes when you can, even if it's a statue of someone who's been gone for more than half a century.

On Saturdays in the fall when the Hawks have a home game, these are the state's five largest cities: Des Moines, Cedar Rapids, Davenport, Sioux City and Kinnick Stadium.

Nile stands at the front door like a grand ambassador of a sport and a university and a state while some 70,000 folks scurry to and fro. Sometimes people do stop for photos at his feet. Sometimes people brace against him to keep from falling down, drunk. Always his eyes are fixed above and beyond them on the unreachable horizon of what used to be and might have been.

The cramped seating may have been contributory to the salty language that ensued right from the opening kickoff and rose to deafening levels whenever any one of three things occurred: a penalty flag thrown against the Hawkeyes, a successful play executed by the other team or an unsuccessful play executed by Iowa.

Max seemed a little nonplussed by the sporting vocabulary he was exposed to at our early events. Football crowds are especially profane, owing possibly to the bloodlust that is endemic to the game. Sometimes I could feel Max looking at me for explanation. It can be a real dilemma. What are one's options? "Don't worry son; they're just inebriated." Or maybe, "That fella's just being obnoxious 'cuz it's a football game - you know, something really important!" A real longshot might have been, "Guess what, Max? I used to act like that too, before you came along."

As a matter of fact, I was then still spending much time at a workplace where ribald language was the norm. As a saloonkeeper I was fluent in the street vernacular and employed it freely. Nevertheless, a self-imposed censorship came upon me quite naturally when children started decorating my life. It was effortless really and I felt as self-conscious cursing within earshot of other people's kids as I did my own.

I don't think Max expected me to shush the masses, but I wonder if he wondered why I was so anxious to bring him there.

The halftime pageantry perhaps. From our vantage point, 46 rows up in section U; parallel with the back of the south end zone in the east stands, the deployment of the marching band was quite a spectacle. The ranks assembled at the end of the field opposite us like a regimented colony of ants. As they strutted into position the drum major and baton twirler burst forth like royal insects doing some elaborate rite of pre-mating choreography. It's all very impressive, an element of the college game that is sorely lacking at the professional level. The show always culminates with 70,000 people on their feet clapping and reverently singing the Iowa Fight Song: "What's the word? Fight, fight, fight. The word is fight, fight, fight for Iowa; let every loyal Iowan sing…until the game is won."

The Hawkeyes hung on to win this one by a final score of 21-20. Max and I were 2-0.

Closer to Home

Max's rookie year as a patron of the sports was rounded out when Iowa came to Des Moines on December 3, 1996 to take on the hometown Drake Bulldogs in college basketball.

The venue was the Knapp Center, a cozy, on-campus gym that opened in 1992. This outing required no planes or trains; barely even an automobile. Drake's campus is just a couple of miles from our neighborhood.

When I was a boy Drake was playing its home basketball games downtown in Veteran's Memorial Auditorium, more commonly referenced as Vet's, or occasionally, The Barn.

I saw the Bulldogs' Wayne Kreklow pour in 43 points there one night, making 19 of 22 shots from the floor, most of them from a distance that would now count for a point more than they did then.

Same thing the night Larry Bird rang up 45 as the star of the visitors from Indiana State, most of those rained in during a second half display of long range shooting virtuosity.

One night I remember Drake upsetting a nationally ranked team - I think it was Tulsa - when a missed free throw was fought for and the ball somehow bounced off the floor into the basket to register the deciding points.

Drake had some memorable teams during the tenure of their most fondly remembered coach, Maury John, whose best seasons coincided with my adolescence. In 1969 the David from the Midwest nearly slew the Goliath that was UCLA, then in the midst of a run of consecutive national championships that would reach the count of eight. The plucky Bulldogs finally succumbed in the national semifinals by a mere three points. Then they trounced another perennial powerhouse, North Carolina, in a consolation game that really did offer some consolation to those of us who believed in the unlikely team from the small school in Des Moines.

By the time I took Max to see his first college basketball game, I was attending as an Iowa alum, and so, not even rooting for the hometown team that night. After all, the Hawkeyes too fielded some storied squads when I was a boy. "Sudden" Sam Williams and "Downtown" Freddie Brown were colorful favorites of mine.

The great 1969-70 Hawkeyes, coached by the sandpapery Ralph Miller, went through their Big Ten conference season undefeated. That team averaged in excess of 100 points per game in an era that preceded adoption of the three-point field goal and a shot clock.

Only a fluke basket by someone grandiosely named Pembrook Burrows III playing for Jacksonville kept that Iowa team from advancing to the Final Four the year after Drake had been there. Ten years later another Iowa team did make it that far.

On the night that Max and I went to the Knapp Center there was no such greatness on display. My alma mater won the game easily, 79-59. But they vanquished a sorry opponent that was in the early stages of what was to become a historically bad 2-26 season - 0 for18 in the Missouri Valley Conference - and segue into a barely better 3-24 log the following year. That two-year 5-50 stretch would mark the low point of a program that was generally prouder than such embarrassing numbers would entitle.

Besides the game itself, the markedly different ambience than what we'd experienced at baseball and football venues was noteworthy.

Midweek college basketball games do not lend themselves to the sort of pre-game tailgating that's so much a part of college football Saturdays. People often eat supper at home before the game; the hot dog really has no place here. And there aren't the legions of beermen roaming campus arenas on winter evenings that you'll find deployed in the grandstands and bleachers wherever, whenever the summer game is being professionally played.

Those factors mitigate against the formation of a lynch mob when a refereed travesty is imposed upon the home team and its fans. Unfortunately they're offset because officials have to make lots of split-second judgment calls, many of them while on the run trying to keep up with the rapid pace of the game. We suppose the refs do the best they can, such as that may be, but it's never good enough. In college basketball too, there is inevitably that loud chorus of speech freed from the constraints of civility, the primal jeer of the masses in outcry against whatever rules them. It's what makes the gyms rock and lets everyone with a ticket feel momentarily as though they might actually loose the chains that bind them; that they might throw off their meek obedience and take charge and lead whomever dares follow them to a better place.

Then there's a TV timeout and everyone clamors for the cheerleaders to *PLEEEEEEZE* aim the t-shirt bazooka at them while the remote controlled mini-zeppelin festooned with advertisements takes flight through the arena for the airborne branch of the sensory invasion that now routinely launches at every lull in the action of American sporting contests.

Since I'd played all three of the major American sports as a schoolboy, I remained interested in watching them as a washed-up, middle aged never-was. But from the start I think Max was more interested in watching me than the games when I took him afield for father-son maneuvers. If he wasn't necessarily drawn to the spectacle of athletic competition he was certainly drawn to me. I knew nothing of hunting, fishing, home repairs or the commercial arts like negotiation. Sports were it; I had to play to what I saw as my strengths.

When me and the kid shuffled from the sweaty pungence of the Knapp Center out into the cold December dryness we'd been emotionally inseparable teammates for more than five years. But we were still getting acquainted in important ways. I didn't yet know the difference between finding out who kids are and steering them towards who you might've liked to be.

Good Day for a Movie

I didn't see *Star Wars* when it was first released in 1977. Eventually I gave it a look when it came to the Plantation Drive-In. It was a good film to see from the comfort of your car while passing joints around, but even in that relaxed milieu I didn't really think much of it. I'd never caught the *Star Trek* fever either. Real life outer space adventure had always fascinated me but neither science nor fiction drew much more of my attention separately than did the two in combination.

Even so, when *Star Wars* was re-released with a 20th anniversary marketing angle in 1997 I got swept up in the excitement. I saw it as a perfect opportunity for Max and I to escape the mid-winter doldrums and also as something of a challenge just to score a couple of tickets for an opening weekend matinee.

STUBS

The film was showing at River Hills, downtown between the Des Moines River and Vet's Auditorium. At the time it was the biggest cinema auditorium in the state. Now it's defunct, having been razed to make room for the Wells Fargo Arena which has replaced Vet's as the major event venue in these parts.

I threw myself into the large crowd that gathered outside early on a January Saturday morning to buy tickets for that afternoon's showing. The queue was as long as the weather was cold. I saw a neighbor there, getting tickets [I presumed] for herself, her husband and their son who is the same age as Max. We hailed one another from distant sectors of the mob.

Eventually I reached the ticket window and managed two for later that same day. I returned home like a hunter back from the field. My recounting of the hand-to-hand at the box office stoked the fire of anticipation in Max. After what I'd been through I was even persuading myself that the movie was going to be better than I'd thought upon first viewing. The Dolby surround sound would be a major upgrade from the scratchy window-mounted speaker at the drive-in and maybe being high had dulled rather than sharpened my senses the first time around.

We headed back to River Hills after lunch in a spirit of adventure, leaving the wife and small children safely at home. Now the amoeboid throng outside was a mix of those too late to have any hope of a matinee and other, more farsighted fans lining up for evening showings. As for us, we proceeded in through the door reserved for the VIP's already in possession of tickets.

Finally having wrested popcorn, candy and soda from the food riots at the concessions counter in the lobby, we forged ahead into the vast seating area and staked out a couple on an aisle. The place was filling fast and I had the idea that perhaps we ought to save seats for our neighbors. I assumed she'd been buying tickets that morning for the same show, though I didn't know that for certain. I scanned the auditorium and didn't see them. We fended off several squatters as the available seating rapidly dwindled and a mood of excitement steadily escalated. A concert atmosphere was gathering. Soon the management was canvassing the crowd in search of empty seats.

"Are those three taken?" I was asked by an imperious man about my age, dressed in the full regalia of a double-breasted, oversized jacket with gold buttons, brocade and epaulets. He gestured towards the adjacent chairs with his standard issue flashlight as though wielding a light saber.

"We're saving them," I explained between munches of made-too-soon, poorly buttered, exorbitantly priced popcorn.

"You can't save seats," came the edict from the dark side of the flashlight. "Are the people here?"

"Yes," I said reflexively. "They're out getting treats."

That pale lie bought us the time it would take for the Master of Cinema to make a lap of the auditorium. Surely our neighbors would arrive by then. But they didn't. When the keeper-of-the-thermostat returned he was visibly harried and seemed to be losing control of a round of musical chairs playing out on a grand scale.

"I'm gonna have to take those seats," he decreed as whiffs of in-justice filled my flaring nostrils.

"No!" I rebelled. "I stood in line all morning outside in the cold. They'll be here any minute!"

We volleyed. He went for the kill. To the utter amazement of my five year-old son, I was threatened with arrest! As a final, desperate ploy I begged for the chance to go out and check the lobby. I was granted a brief reprieve. Frantically I looked for them in the treat mob while I plugged coins into the lobby pay phone [a primitive device once used for the placement of private phone calls in public places] and called their home. Someone finally answered. What? Not coming! Tonight's showing! Bail me out? Never mind! Click...

I guess the movie was alright as anti-climaxes go. On the way home I explained to Max about how they used to show Bugs Bunny cartoons before the main feature.

Alone Again

1998 was a baseball season for the ages.

A baby-faced Cub rookie named Kerry Wood tied a major league record by striking out 20 Houston Astros on a cold, drizzly day in April at Wrigley Field in a performance that ranks with the most dominating pitching performances of all-time [consider that

Wood was only a scratch single from a perfect game and that over three quarters of the 27 outs required no fielders besides Wood and his catcher].

As the season evolved it would be defined by the home run derby waged all summer between the Cubs' Sammy Sosa and the Cardinals' Mark McGwire.

Sosa hit 20 in the month of June alone, a total that used to represent a good season's work, and any ball that McGwire got airborne seemed destined for the seats.

The Cubs and Cardinals started drawing good crowds even for pre-game batting practice. It made for good theatre, the happy Dominican slugger and the bashful redheaded basher personifying the long-standing rivalry between their respective teams and cities. Their personal duel was like a good horse race, McGwire breaking way in front only to have Sosa draw up on his shoulder as the season headed for the stretch, the two of them separating from the rest of the pack, going neck-and-neck at a record pace.

Meanwhile, almost lost in the background was the increasing likelihood as the season waned that the Cubs would qualify for the post-season playoffs, something that was rare in the organization's long and mostly mediocre history.

They almost blew it by losing six of their last eight games and allowing the San Francisco Giants to squeeze into the picture. The two teams started play on the last day of the regular season tied for the final playoff berth. The Cubs were playing the Astros in Houston; the Giants were facing the Rockies in Denver.

The Giants burst out to a 7-0 lead. The Cubs were struggling in Texas, unable to muster much offense now at the very end of a season marked by homers - lots of them. Sosa managed a run-scoring single early in the final game, but nothing more emphatic than that as the Cubs coughed up a 3-1 lead and a deadlocked game and season extended nervously into the overtime of extra innings.

Simultaneously the Rockies, with nothing to play for, nevertheless were mounting a comeback against the Giants that was unlikely, even by the high-scoring standards of Coors Field, situated as it was in the rarefied altitude of the mountains which was known for giving an extra wing to airborne baseballs.

Just after the Cubs lost their game in the bottom of the 11th and retreated to their clubhouse, Neifi Perez, hardly a slugger, cracked a game-winning homer for the Rockies in Denver.

The Cubs and Giants, like two ordinary children being rewarded for participation in a race neither could win, would meet the following evening in Chicago in a one-game playoff to get into the playoffs.

As the self-appointed delegate for my immediate and extended family, I insisted upon being there. With the tribe's blessing but no ticket I left home on the morning of Monday, September 28, 1998, bound for Chicago. I'd scrambled a one-night reservation at a downtown hotel and reasoned that I'd scalp a ticket on the streets outside the ballpark once I arrived on the scene.

It was silly. I was going to an awful lot of trouble and expense for what? A chance to watch a couple of clumsy girls stumble down the runway in the bathing suit competition? The Cubs and Giants had both backed into this dramatic scenario but still, it did have the power to conjure memories of Bobby Thompson's "shot heard 'round the world;" the game-winning, pennant-winning homer that decided the playoff between the Giants and Dodgers when both teams were still in New York in 1951.

The ratios were all wrong. I would spend 10 hours on the road so I could see a three-hour ballgame. It would cost me as much to park my car overnight as it would to fuel it; as much, in other words, to not drive it as to drive it. I would pay a full day's rate for a downtown hotel despite that I'd need it no longer than a furtive, illicit couple would require some privacy at a sleazy motel on the outskirts.

Still, it was a giddy morning's drive from Des Moines to Chicago. I arrived several hours in advance of the 7:05 P.M. game time, parked the car, checked into the hotel, stowed my toiletries and a change of clothes and headed for the Harrison St. train station to catch the 'L' north to Wrigley Field.

As soon as I disembarked at Addison Street I was engulfed in a carnival atmosphere as palpable as weather. Wrigleyville has become a Mecca for Cub pilgrims who swarm there seasonally and overwhelm regular folks who live their rank and file lives in the neighborhood.

Of course, much is paid for the privilege of visiting the shrine. In this rare case I was prepared to pay exorbitantly to get inside the temple that night. Wrigley Field is built where a seminary once stood, something I first learned when I read it on a souvenir beer cup. It remains a training ground for leaders of a bizarre, illogical faith.

I don't recall the hastily arranged means for distribution of tickets to a game that was scheduled with less than 24 hours' notice. Essentially there was a run on the stadium box office at dawn and the not quite 40,000 seats were purchased well before I hit town at lunchtime. Many were bought by speculators who now roamed in droves. I would have my ticket; it was simply a question of how much it would cost. I tried to play on the sympathies of street vendors, a decidedly unsympathetic lot, with tales of my 700 mile round trip pilgrimage. None gave a damn. I grew impatient as the time to open the gates approached. I wanted to get inside as soon as I could and start soaking up a historic night at a historic venue.

A collegiate looking threesome strolled past waving four tickets aloft in advertisement, fanned like a hand of cards.

"How much for one?" I wondered aloud, trying to affect the air of a dispassionate pollster.

"One-fifty!" said the one gripping the merchandise.

"I've only got a hundred," I hardballed.

"One-fifty!" he countered, this time even more emphatically.

"I had to drive 350 miles to be here," I whined.

"From where?" he cracked; my foot was in the door.

"Des Moines...Iowa," I told him in the self-deprecating cadence of a native who'd learned to assume others' poor command of U.S. capitals.

"Des Moines! Man, my girlfriend goes to Drake! Come on man, let him have it for a hundred. He drove a thousand miles!" exhorted one of the ticketmaster's pals. The other one would join in too, and together the three of us prevailed on the better nature of the ringleader and brought him to his knees. He accepted my crisp c-note in exchange for a ticket with a face value of $14.00. We agreed to meet again inside, the trio of frat brothers further pitying me on the grounds that I was traveling alone and deciding to gift me with their fellowship for no extra charge.

Once ticketed I headed for the turnstiles and entered the ballpark driven by an emotional hodgepodge of reverence, excitement and anticipation.

My assigned seat was in a "terrace reserved" section on the main level; beneath the upper deck and parallel to the left-field line in section 215. But the gates had just opened and the first injection of fans was allowed to roam the cathedral freely. I headed down near the Cub dugout and watched the players milling around the cage during batting practice.

Then I was struck by the monolithic abacus of a scoreboard that looms beyond center-field. In a ballpark routinely exited by home run balls aimed to left and right fields, the scoreboard that's operated by men inside of it like a contraption from Oz remains the only outdoor spot on the hallowed premises where no baseball has ever gone. During the season every big league game scheduled on a given day is laid out inning by inning. But on this night the huge green chalkboard was blank except for the names of these two teams that were happy to be staying after school.

The Cubs wrote on the board first when the beak-nosed Gary Gaetti, a mid-season acquisition who'd been discarded by the Minnesota Twins, repaid the team that plucked him from the scrap heap with a two-run homer in the third inning. This prompted my frat pals to offer me some of my ticket money back in the form of a beer. When I declined they instead offered me all I cared to eat from the large bag of pistachios they'd brought along.

Pitching for the Cubs in this biggest game of the long season was Steve Trachsel, known in some quarters as "The Human Rain Delay."

The first time I saw him pitch was in Des Moines at Sec Taylor Stadium when he toiled for the Iowa Cubs as a prospect rising through the ranks of the Chicago farm system. He was so methodical as to erase all appreciation that he was engaged in an athletic activity. His pace was sloth-like; there was an intermission between pitches commensurate with what one might expect between moves at a high-level chess match. God forbid anyone should get on base and give him more to reckon with than just the batter.

Trachsel's deliberate rhythms seemed to hypnotize the Giants' hitters on a night when over-eagerness would have been understandable. Even though six of them were sufficiently discriminating and patient to draw bases on balls, Trachsel took the mound for the top of the seventh inning with a no-hitter and a 4-0 lead.

Whenever he clogged the bases with walks the hyper, nervous crowd exhorted him to bear down as though trying to midwife the birth of a victory.

With one out in the seventh the secondary pressure of the no-hitter was relieved when one of the Giants lined a single to right. Trachsel's night was over. If only as a consequence of the sheer importance of the contest he must surely have broken a jersey-soaking sweat, notwithstanding the somnolent pace of his labors. He left to a deafening two-part roar that both appreciated his efforts and celebrated that the game might now be decided before the date changed.

The Cubs withstood a too little-too late rally by the Giants in the top of the ninth. When flagrantly mustachioed reliever Rod Beck induced Joe Carter to pop out to Cub first-baseman Mark Grace for the last out of the game, all heaven broke loose at Wrigley Field. The players briefly repaired to the privacy of their club-house only to return armed with magnums of champagne which they used to hose down the fans closest to the field.

The game had lasted three hours and forty-one minutes; an inordinately long time for a regulation, relatively low-scoring [5-3] ballgame. Chalk it up to Trachsel's monogram.

It was the Cubs' 90th win of the season and their last. They were quickly dispatched by the Atlanta Braves who swept them out of the playoffs in the minimum three games before that week was over.

The day following the game, the only one allowed for the Cubs to travel and reground themselves before meeting the Braves, I checked out of my hotel and drove home early in the morning. My former self rode shotgun.

There had been a long time in my life when I would have been ill-advised to make such a trip alone. I was not to be trusted with myself. Even in the company of friends obliged to double as chaperones, I pushed my luck more than once in a city I was no match for, especially when drunk. The Cubs had won and so, in another sense, had I. To have sprayed and guzzled champagne in celebration of my small personal victory would have been to undo it. Instead I cruised under control westward and thought that I might like to do this again sometime.

New York, New York

E arly in 1999 the lure of cheap airfare that had sent Max and I winging to Chicago struck again. This time the availability of round trips to New York City for a hundred bucks gave me an idea as spousally romantic as Opening Day at Wrigley Field with my first-born child had been in a filial way.

I planned a 24 hour date that would serve the dual purpose of celebrating my birthday.

Chris and I flew to New York early on the morning of Saturday, February 27. We had lunch in a Manhattan Deli; outlandishly sized and priced pastrami sandwiches. We strolled and shopped; I bought a pair of Cole Haans on sale somewhere that I can still wear because I wear them so seldom.

That night we had dinner at Sardi's. I can't recall the meal itself so much as the bustle of the restaurant. Besides the walking, talking crowd the walls too were crowded with photos and caricatures of luminaries who'd dined there over the years.

After dinner we went to the Eugene O'Neill Theatre on W. 49th ST. to see Brian Dennehy as Willie Loman in *Death of a Salesman*. It's the only show I've ever seen on Broadway and it was spellbinding. The theatre itself was elegant if a bit cramped and I remember feeling myself something of a poser, imagining that the rest of the audience did this as often as I did ballgames.

The contrast between live theatre and sports was stark. There was no booing of Dennehy or the rest of the cast. I heard not a single discouraging or four-letter word even so much as uttered, let alone hollered. Coincidentally, neither did I notice anybody working the crowd harnessed to a tray full of beers.

Dennehy and the supporting players hit lots of home runs but my unstaged eye caught nary an error on anyone's part. Granted, I attended as a Midwestern tourist, not a critic, and my patronage of the arts was still rather nouveau at that time. I was predisposed to be awestruck, but the reviews of the show were generally in accord with my personal assessment of it, minus the compare/contrast with an evening spent at a ballpark.

When the curtain calls finally subsided into the dull throb of too clapped hands we were flushed out into the streets and the New York night. Chris and I walked along, lost in the moment and out of our element, when we were abruptly forced to the curb by an oncoming couple. They didn't seem to be enjoying their evening as much as we were. Not only that, but they looked an awful lot like… did you see who I saw? It was Alec Baldwin and Kim Basinger.

Provincial reflexes took hold of us and we turned in pursuit of our celebrity counterparts.

"Hey, Baldsinger! Wait up! Can we buy you guys a drink? Can we get some directions? Don't worry - we don't carry a camera! Know anyplace with good karaoke? Do you swing? Listen, if you're ever in Des Moines, drop in my joint on Ingersoll and tell 'em Mike sencha…"

They rounded the corner up ahead at a brisk clip and we, taking the hint, pulled over. So it was true, all that we'd heard back home about rude New Yorkers. Just as well; Chris didn't think as much of Alec as I did of Kim anyway. It never would have worked. So instead we returned to our hotel where I redeemed the brownie points I'd racked up for masterminding the weekend's itinerary.

Chris and I were almost ten years married and had three kids to show for it. Then, as now and right from the start, I don't think I understood why she loved me as much as she clearly did and still does. Sometimes I feel myself cared about in a way that is both reassuring and guilt-inducing. It seems on a scale I'm not able to reciprocate.

What leaks have sprung in the dike we've built against a relentless world have been mostly my workmanship, and it's been mostly hers that's plugged them.

If there are places still in me that are either very cold or very hot, I do not as often go to them since she agreed to take me on.

Sober when we met, I resumed drinking during our courtship and continued to for the first several years of our marriage. Sometimes Chris drank with me. Sometimes she looked out for me while I drank. Sometimes she just looked for me. And finally she pleaded that I stop - for the good of all concerned. It was easier begged than done, but it has happened nonetheless.

I stay out of bars and my darker corners these days but I haven't forgotten where they are. I whistle past them all the time.

The next morning we arose and flew away, back to our real lives.

A Star is Born?

The occasion of my next visit to the theatre was a Sunday matinee at the Des Moines Civic Center in November of 1999. My companion was again Max. The show was *Jekyll & Hyde*.

We sat rather near the stage in Row C, left of center in seats 29 and 30. At intermission we browsed the lobby souvenir stand and Max selected an ink pen designed to look like a hypodermic needle.

During the second act his eyes widened as the plot thickened. This time it was more father watching son than the other way around. When the show was over and we made our way out of the Civic Center, Max insisted on stopping again at the souvenir booth, this time for a CD of the show's music.

He was by then a member of a children's community choral group, having been referred to it by a fellow chorister from the cherub choir at our church. And he'd already developed the habit of sorting baseball cards in his room while listening to Ella Fitzgerald and Louie Armstrong CD's, courtesy of his Aunt Sue. He was a music man from a young age and we were beginning to wonder if perhaps there had been more to his prophecy as a four year-old watching the Super Bowl halftime show than any of us had guessed at that time.

Now he took the soundtrack CD home and memorized the title characters' solos, belting them out while sketching crude portraits of his baseball heroes, using their cards as models. The cheap hypodermic pen soon broke but the music played over and over.

About a month later Max's choir performed a holiday concert on the same Civic Center stage where Dr. Jekyll had morphed into Mr. Hyde. The crowd was not as large when Max sang his brief solo as the angel Gabriel as it had been the last time we were there, but it was a potentially daunting circumstance nonetheless; especially, I thought, for an eight year-old. But he knocked it out of the auditorium. I was understandably proud, but equally fascinated. From whence had come this poise? It certainly was not his father's to pass on.

There had begun in me a broadening of the horizon, much of it now at the hands of a young boy I lived with. In exchange for my rants and ramblings on the finer points and goings-on of the sporting world I was being gradually shown the way to alternative recreations that mesmerized me in ways that no ballgame could. A game that ended on a play at the plate was still hard to beat and cause for primal screaming, but silent weeping brought on by live theatre was felt more deeply and surely as therapeutic.

Something happened to me when my father-in-law gave us tickets to see *Les Miserables* as a Christmas gift in 1991. We saw it in Des Moines in early 1992, a second time in London in the summer of 1993 and a third time later in that decade in Iowa City. The first time I heard the song, "I Dreamed a Dream," I shook from the inside out and realized my interests to that point had been much too narrow.

Now, that emotional temblor was shaking the house where we lived.

Kansas City, Here We Come

Later in that winter of 1999 the Cubs announced their schedule for the 2000 season. Thanks to baseball commissioner Bud Selig's brainchild of inter-league play, they were slated for a series in Kansas City in July. This was cause for jubilation.

STUBS

Kansas City is half the distance from Des Moines that Chicago is. Tickets to Royals games are cheap and plentiful. Kauffman Stadium is no Wrigley Field, but it's nice by the low standards of post-1950/pre-1990 American stadium architecture, and handily positioned practically on the shoulder of the interstate highway system.

In March of 2000, before the baseball season officially launched in April, I unofficially launched it in our household by purchasing five Club Box seats on the 1st baseline @ $17.00 per for the game between the Cubs and Royals on Sunday, July 16, 2000. The whole family was going! Some of us appreciated this prospect just slightly more than others. I was the spokesman for that contingent [*The Fans* - me, Max and Ben]. It didn't seem right somehow that our traveling companions [*The Indifferents* - Chris and Emma] would have seats as good as ours, but such is family egalitarianism.

By the time July finally arrived the little league seasons were already over for Max and Ben.

Ben had frolicked through tee-ball, glad at last to be allowed onto the field of play instead of being dragged to his big brother's games to merely watch.

Max, at nine, had completed his first season of full-fledged, let's keep score & kick their asses baseball. He'd been randomly assigned to a team that turned out to be quite good. I can remember just one loss, after which one of the team's two coaches gathered the boys in their dugout. He'd noticed some pouty helmet-tossing and carping about the umps springing up in the ranks as it became clear that this was not the Rockies'day. He rightly wanted to nip the bad attitudes in the bud.

"Boys," he intoned to the captive audience arrayed end-to-end on the bench in front of him, "I noticed some temper tantrums out there today and I hate to see that." He went on with a stirring monologue about sportsmanship and valor, occasionally invoking names of major league stars recalled from his own boyhood to further a point. At length he summed up the lecture with what he thought a rhetorical query that, "you don't see the big leaguers tossing their bats and helmets and crying at the umpires, do you?"

He'd broken the old lawyers' axiom about never asking a question unless you're sure of what the answer will be.

"Yes you do!" one of the best players and loudest whiners begged to differ. Class dismissed.

Max was a fringe player on a team well-stocked with budding ballplayers. His season had gotten off to a painfully ignominious start when he took a hardball flush in the chops at one of the team's early practices. Undaunted, he threw himself at the game, trying as hard, I'm sure, to impress his dad as he did to impress his coaches and peers. He did impress me too, though not with a bat or a ball or a glove, or in any of the ways that mattered to him then.

It was 106 in Kansas City at game time on July 16, according to one of those revolving clock/thermometers at a local bank. This made everyone in our traveling party uncomfortable, particularly *The Indifferents* who became *The Reluctants*. Luckily we were seated in a section shielded from direct sunlight. It was barely 100 in the club boxes. Things got even cooler for us Cub fans when Sammy Sosa, on his way to another Ruthian home run total that year, cranked out a couple just for us in pacing the visitors to victory.

Given the oppressive heat and the larger than normal crowd drawn by the Royals' opposition, I wouldn't have been surprised by a riotous run on the stadium's famous fountains that sprayed refreshingly and colorfully beyond the outfield walls between the left and right field bleachers. Instead a lone and apparently delirious refugee from the 70's leaped over the left-field fence in the late innings and headed for the infield - buck naked!

I'd never seen 2nd base stolen from the left-field seats, but this fellow got a good jump on the security team. He very likely could have gone in standing up and been safe, however briefly, before being removed to the county "bullpen." And since he didn't even leave on his jockstrap and cup when he stripped down for the dash, he should have gone in feet first if he insisted on sliding. Better a strawberry on the rump than a...than the alternative. But he went in like Pete Rose. It's usually called a headfirst slide, or sometimes a belly flop, but no one there was thinking in terms of either the guy's head or his belly. It was one of those unscripted teachable moments.

"You see boys;" I told Max and Ben solemnly, "that's a good example of why most good baseball coaches say you should always slide feet first - too much risk of injury the other way..."

Sweet Home Des Moines

There are three stubs in my box from the game at Wrigley Field between the Cubs and Cardinals on August 14, 2000. I have no specific memories of it. The number of tickets suggests that it was Max, Ben and me, the family's baseball stooges/musketeers, that attended the game, but the date's proximity to our wedding anniversary hints that I sold Chris on the trip to Chicago as some sort of romantic extravaganza involving the whole family.

Sometimes our Chicago itinerary was a mix of group sightseeing, stags at Wrigley Field and girls-only hikes up and down the Magnificent Mile. This may have been that sort of tour.

I tried some research on the date in hopes of jogging my memory. The Cubs won the game, 7-3. We apparently saw Sosa hit his 37th homer of the year after witnessing #'s 26 & 27 about a month prior in Kansas City. I'm sure we did some "ballhawking" during pregame batting practice out on Waveland Avenue behind the left-field bleachers; that was customary. A pack forms before every home game to scrap for balls clouted clear out to the street. Mostly it's made up of devout tourists like us, but there is a core of savvy locals with scouts in the bleachers to give them headstarts in a ball's direction. The veteran outfielders of the streets thus get the best jumps and most of the balls. But no one really goes away empty-handed. There is at least a sense of having been included in a ritual that is long-standing and worthwhile, not to mention free.

Our Terrace Reserved seats in section 236 cost $16.00 each. Today those seats for a game in August versus the Cardinals would go for $40.00, assuming you didn't have to get them in the "secondary market."

More interesting was my discovery that, on that same date, a game in Little Falls, New Jersey between the New Jersey Jackals and the Catskill Cougars of the Northern League was delayed at the outset for a record seven hours and six minutes by rain. Then the scheduled matinee was finally played [Cougars beat the Jackals, 6-1], ending after 11:00 P.M. Almost poetically, the game was played at Yogi Berra Stadium. One can imagine the ballpark marquee shouting, "Get Your Tickets Now For Afternoon Game Last Night!" or words to that effect...

Actually I have more and better memories of the 2000 season stashed at our home ballpark in Des Moines.

Name me a team besides the 2000 edition of the Iowa Cubs that had four unrelated players on the roster with last names starting with Z. Julio Zuleta, Carlos Zambrano, Alan Zinter and Dave Zancanaro were all part of a team that made its way to the league basement and snoozed the summer away - ZZZZ...

Me and the boys adopted the scrappy infield duo of Chad Meyers and Augie Ojeda as our favorites. They were both undersized hustlers and if the team had fared better I would have dubbed it, The Chad 'n Augie Choo-Choo. As it was they finished up the track with a record of 57-87.

In those days I was the proprietor of a thriving public house and we had season tickets every year squarely behind home plate, just a few rows back from the playing field. We were in the section where visiting scouts sat with their radar guns and stopwatches, rendering in numbers for the benefit of those not present what they saw with their eyes and felt in their hearts about the players they watched.

Sometimes the pitcher assigned to start the following day's game would sit near us, charting pitches as part of the preparation for his next outing. Zambrano then was a man-child, listed in the program as a teenager. He was bound for the big leagues and he looked the part with massive thighs and buns and hands like the paws of a big cat. Sometimes in between innings kids would pester him for autographs and he would usually oblige by scribbling his signature on caps and mitts like a too-busy doctor scrawling out illegible prescriptions for patients sick with hero worship.

He was a scared Venezuelan kid then, far from home and out of his element. Now he's a bona fide major league character, as likely to entertain the fans with his antics as his pitching arm. He's making $18 million per season and his autograph isn't so easy to come by as it was in Des Moines at the turn of the century.

Then, as now, Des Moines was the smallest market in the country that was home to a Triple A baseball team. If the players were only a strained oblique muscle from the big leagues we too were closer than the 350 miles that separate Des Moines and Chicago. In fact we were as close as our seats were to the diamond. We heard pitches sizzle into the catcher's mitt at 95 MPH and saw them veer like Blue Angels breaking formation. We watched the arcs of balls blasted 400+ feet in the general direction of the dome of the state capitol that looms beyond center field like the remote but visible golden ball of the big leagues. It glistens out there on the horizon when days come to dusk and ballgames come to the middle innings.

It's good to live in a place where baseball is played professionally and it's an added bonus for us that the local team is a branch of the major league one that will always be our favorite.

There is an ambition still at work in the minor leagues that nowadays sometimes degrades into complacency upon promotion and achievement of the multi-million dollar contracts that are commonplace for established big leaguers. Winning and losing happen more at an individual level in the minors - a few make it; most don't. It's nice if the home team wins, but hardly necessary. What I most like to see is players who play like I used to - all out, with hustle. That's what should be featured on ESPN highlight shows; hustle. Instead they show prima donnas lingering at the plate in admiration of their own work. Minor leaguers growl; major leaguers burp.

The ballpark in Des Moines used to be called Sec Taylor Stadium. It was named after a sportswriter of all things, as strong an indicator as I can imagine that relations between the sporting press and the objects of their attentions didn't used to be so adversarial as they've since become. Anyway, the place got all spiffed up in 1992 by the same company that built Camden Yards in Baltimore and a batch of other big league venues and later the team's ownership sold the naming rights. Now it's alliteratively known as Principal Park. The diamond inside is officially named Sec Taylor Field. The facts that the premises include a playground inside the gates which requires a separate admission than the game itself and that the team has a mascot named Cubbie Bear to further amuse children by distracting their attention from baseball are demerits I've gotten used to.

Back in 2000 Max and Ben were too small for me to let them wander off to the playground even if they'd wanted to. I don't even think this was yet the year when I'd bring them home from the ballpark and announce to their mother that they'd soloed to the concession stand and - cause and effect - the restroom. They were both still comfortable with my company in public. We started calling Julio Zuleta "Zulio" and Zambrano, "Zombie" [when he was pitching; not when soliciting his autograph]. We, or at least I, thought it was a natural nickname - close to his real name and an outgrowth of his scariness on the mound – but later when he established himself in Chicago the unimaginative "Big Z" stuck to him. That sounds more like something Zorro might be called at a Mexican brothel.

Ben's level of interest was primarily limited to food, beverage and the fireworks that erupted from the scoreboard whenever the I-Cubs stroked a home run. Max, on the other hand, was becoming a noisemaker and something of a heckler. He was precocious in many ways that ranged from cute to downright impressive, but this emerging trait was not always in that range. Visiting players and umps became regular targets of derision. He'd fire off a wisecrack and then look to me for approval. For awhile I wondered where he was getting his material. Then it dawned that he was just parroting the sort of ballpark vernacular he heard his father spouting.

This wasn't what I wanted to teach about baseball. I wanted to share the nuance like middle infielders cheating towards the bag in double play situations; corner infielders creeping towards the plate when a sacrifice bunt was in order or a speedy hitter was at the plate; the anti-geometry of why a circular and longer path around the bases was faster than the shorter, squared one formed by straight lines between the bases; why zeroes on the scoreboard were called goose eggs.

The finer points would have to wait. First you had to learn the language.

Joyful Noises

W inters are especially long for baseball fans who live in four-season country. Knowing this the brain trust at the helm of the Iowa Cubs launched a January icebreaker, generically called a Fanfest. Fanfests are orgies and pump primers. This one both repaid local fans for past patronage and whetted their appetites for the upcoming season. It was held at the Des Moines Convention Center over a weekend that kicked off with a Friday luncheon and culminated on Sunday, January 21, 2001 with an appearance by Ryne Sandberg, an all-time Cub great who was at the end of a career that would see him enshrined in the Hall of Fame in Cooperstown and his retired jersey #23 fluttering forever from one of the foul poles at Wrigley Field.

We three attended the Sandberg session and I managed to get a sympathetic club official with whom I was casually acquainted through the pub I owned to arrange for autographs on some baseball cards we'd brought along. This freed us from the long queue that formed for less connected idolaters to get their brief audience with the patient but laconic Sandberg who, like most athletes, was more engaging watched from the stands than he is in conversation.

Instead of standing in line while our enthusiasm waned, we roamed the hall and browsed the mix of exhibits and vendors. Young Ben won a baseball trivia contest with me whispering most of the answers to him a la Cyrano DeBergerac. I bought a yellowed copy of the sports page from *The Des Moines Register* edition dated Tuesday, October 8, 1929. The headline announced, "CUBS, MACKS SET FOR SERIES." The "Macks" were the Philadelphia Athletics, owned and managed by the legendary Connie Mack. There was a locally angled story about a very unscientific poll of 22 prominent Des Moines citizens. 12 of them favored the Cubs even though a majority of the dozen thought the A's were the superior team. Opposite that story was an installment of Sec Taylor's column, a comparative analysis of the two teams filed from Chicago on the eve of the Series. Below the fold was a human interest piece gleaned from the wire services about a one-armed man who'd camped out for the first spot in line at Wrigley Field to buy bleacher tickets.

After I got the old paper framed I hung it on the wall at the pub. Now it hangs on the wall at home.

Really the more significant event on our calendar in that winter of 2001 was the concert put on by the St. Olaf College choir at Stephens Auditorium on the campus of Iowa State University in

Ames on Thursday, February 15.

After two years of choral training that established his potential
as a vocal musician, Max had withdrawn the previous fall from
the program with the Des Moines Children's Chorus. Chris and I
suspected that he was leery of a "tour" slated for the end of that
year that amounted to a weekend in Kansas City with overnight
housing in the homes of host families - strangers! We let him sit
the year out rather than force him to sing, but our fingers were
crossed that he'd come back to it for his own reasons.

When I learned that the St. Olaf choir would be touring through
central Iowa I got tickets for the only one in our house who'd been
a student at St. Olaf [me] and the family's best singer [Max]. One
of two exceptional schools that call Northfield, Minnesota home
[Carleton College is also there], St. Olaf runs in my mother's side
of our family like fair skin. She attended there and sang in the
choir that's long been world renowned in a cappella choral cir-
cles. My mother never graduated, though she would have loved
to, and neither did I, deciding early in my one year on the hill that
I would be better suited, if not necessarily as well-served, at the
University of Iowa.

I rarely sing. Usually when I do people either try to politely ignore
me or outright ask that I stop. I've always had a loud voice; it's
just not very melodious. My mother passed to me an appreciation
for a good choir but little else of any harmonic value. I grew up
in a church where the choir was always small and usually earnest
but rarely very good. The choristers were joyful and they were
noisy, attributes which are supposed to be enough to serve God's
musical purposes. We Episcopalians seem generally unconvinced

that the Lord places any premium whatsoever on music. Most of us mumble through hymns like school children of whom the principal has demanded an explanation if we are even moved to shuffle our lips at all. So I still don't like hymns much - unless they're rendered by a group that not only *WANTS* to sing, but *KNOWS HOW*! In that context selections from the hymnal sound downright heavenly.

My ticket to the St. Olaf concert cost $24. Max's cost $12. The disparity in our admission charges was in accordance with widespread pricing principles. But if it is sensible to charge adults and children differently at a restaurant based on the amount of food each age group can be expected to eat, does it make as much sense to reason that adults somehow derive more from entertainment? This is more of a case-by-case proposition. I know I'd like it if tickets were priced this way at Wrigley Field. Maybe I could get in at the big kid rate.

Besides our admissions we bought a couple of CD's in the lobby to take home with us. I got Max a collection of gospel tunes sung by the choir and for myself I selected an episode of Garrison Keillor's radio show, *A Prairie Home Companion*, recorded live at St. Olaf.

I felt the current that runs through me connecting my mother to my children that night in Ames. When I take them to ballgames I feel the one that links them to my dad. Mine is the only flesh those five people will ever meet in. But there are other ways of getting together.

Sing Hallelujah! Play ball!

Time Out

There has been a tendency throughout my life for me to mistake blessings for burdens. That has not been the case with regard to our children. Their innate appeal to me has effectively overridden the conveyor belt stream of responsibility and worry that would be the mumbled side effects if kids were an advertised pharmaceutical [ask your doctor if you're patient enough for parenting activity; children may cause you to pull your hair out, your jaw to drop and result in loss of voice; children can cause an elevation of blood pressure and pains in the neck and ass; consult a physician, pastor, bartender or fellow parent in the event of an argument with your child lasting more than four days; children are not for everyone – people with thin skins, worry warts, little time, active drug addictions and no money should not take children].

There is a magical honeymoon period that goes both ways between parents and kids. For us it would have been from the birth of Max until Emma was maybe three years old, a period of about nine years. During that time all concerned parties could believe in the fairy tale that we were individually and collectively flawless; that there was nothing any one of us or all of us together could not do.

But gradually, inevitably, the truth does out. Superman's real identity is revealed when the kids finally notice Dad uncoiffed and unshaven in his underwear spilling cheerios and springing leaks at the breakfast table. Sometimes he and the saint who sleeps with him even speak crossly to one another. The kids are beautiful and talented, yes, but what's that – a cavity? A 'B'? Damn!

When the sugary dust had all been rubbed from our eyes and settled around us an honest assessment of our prospects was that we might have to settle for our generally kind regard for one another and good health.

We took those terms and ran.

Happy Birthday To Me

R ummaging through the ticket box I found three from a Drake basketball game against Creighton dated February 24, 2001. I turned 47 that day. After being properly feted at home in a ceremony and banquet that included the girls, I took the boys to the Knapp Center where the visiting Bluejays, ranked #23 in the country, methodically vanquished the Bulldogs, 78-70. The subplot of Drake vs. Creighton is Des Moines vs. Omaha. It ain't exactly Big Apple vs. Second City, but it's the best we can do. Score this one for the sophisticates from the Gateway to Oblivion.

I suspect, but can't actually swear to it, that the main event of that weekend for me took place on Friday, February 23rd. That would have been the day that Cubs tickets went on sale for the upcoming season. The last Friday in February has become my ritual of redial and languishing in virtual waiting rooms, relentlessly firing away with my two pea shooters - telephone and computer - at the impregnable vault that is the Cubs' ticketing system. Sooner or later I break through each year on Day One, but by the time I do the fortress is usually looted of the choice summertime seats when preferred opponents, especially the Cardinals, are in town.

After a few hours the tonal jingle of the 11-note phone number pounds the brain like a pile driver and the 20-second clock on the computer monitor becomes a relentlessly repeating countdown to frustration; teasing you over and over into the false hope that your chance, your turn, is imminent while game after game on the home calendar dies and is toe-tagged "SOLD OUT."

By day's end, in one of the great annual ironies of American sport and popular culture, the Cubs, whose hallmarks are defeat and failure, will have sold more tickets at premium prices than they used to sell in an entire season at rates within the means of everyone.

By the next day many of those will already be trading on the secondary market [the euphemism in the ticket trade that is to scalping what gentlemen's club is to strip joint]. It appears that these days there are something more than one of us born every minute.

In the virtual waiting room, just like on the field between the white lines, some years are better than others. In 2001 I had a pretty good year.

2001: A BASE(BALL) ODYSSEY

Friday the 13th; April, 2001: The home opener for the Iowa Cubs. The opponent was the Tucson Sidewinders. Chris and I and the boys were in section M; row 3; seats 1-4. My educated guess is that Emma was left behind with her grandma.

I'd like to say, "There's no superstition in baseball," the way Tom Hanks declared there's no crying, but it ain't so.

It's fair to suppose that the date of our first trip to the ballpark that season wasn't lost on me. Probably not on my companions either since I was by then some sort of jinx in all their eyes.

But any suspicion of bad omens was way off the mark. 2001 turned out as well as any season could without including the Cubs in the World Series.

On May 16th I saw Sammy Sosa hit his 400th career homer from a club box seat only six rows removed from the diamond at Wrigley Field. I traveled alone inasmuch as the game was on a Wednesday night and school was not yet out for the summer.

But as soon as it was we were off to Chicago! The kids' last day of school was Wednesday, June 6. The next day we were in Chicago to see the Cubs take on the Cardinals.

The end of the school year coincided pretty closely with the end of the little league season. That year Max had been a member of the Raccoon Valley Cubs and I had been the team's coach. I don't know what our record was - seems to me we lost a couple more than we won - but man we had a helluva band! In subsequent years roughly half of that team would garner high school All-State recognition as a musician of one sort or another.

I had no idea how to teach a kid to hit or catch or throw. I did understand the rules and strategic protocols far better than any of the players so I managed a bare level of credibility and some fun was had. There were but two rules that I can recall: 1] any explicit request as to position or placement in the lineup was automatically refused and 2] everyone had to have a nickname bestowed by me.

All that was left of our Raccoon Valley season was the last game when we made our family road trip to celebrate the end of the school year.

This time our tickets were in 101A, the so-called "Family Section" of the left-field bleachers where alcohol was neither sold nor otherwise allowed unless smuggled in via someone's bloodstream. This small dry island in the upper left-hand corner of an ocean of beer was an especially prime location during batting practice. It cost more than ballhawking on Wavelend Avenue, yes, but more balls landed in the bleachers than beyond them and there was also the significant advantage of being able to see the ball off the bat as opposed to scanning the sky for incoming missiles on the street outside.

We staked out positions while the visiting Cardinals were still taking their cuts.

The vistas at Wrigley Field are beautiful because they are essentially just enclosed arrangements of organic, natural elements. Gulls bob and glide between rests on the guy wires strung tautly all the way from the foul poles to the screen behind home plate. Their erratic flight patterns swoop down from the blues and whites of the sky and passerby clouds to the fluttering deep green vines that soften, if only to the eye, the tall brick outer boundaries of the playing field. From there your attention draws horizontally across the shallower but brighter shade of the vast outfield grass and the tanned clay of the infield.

Later the grounds crew reddens the infield dirt with a hose and lays down the bright white pinstripes of the baselines that leave home together and end up as far apart as the deepest corners of left and right field. The whole majestic scene is polka-dotted with the colored caps and uniforms of the players and it is only the frequent but irregular finger snaps of bats on balls and balls in gloves that keep one's head above total immersion in the sheer grandeur of the premises.

An organ somewhere in the upper reaches lays down an upbeat meter for the poem that will recite itself on the panoramic stage by day's end. No dirges come from it; not even on those all too frequent days of loss. This place is silver-lined, yet another way that it is church-like, besides that clergy once trained on these same grounds.

The games themselves are in the same proportion to the table they're served upon as a Thanksgiving feast is to its preparation. After they're finished the gulls descend on the grounds en masse. Depending on one's mood after a loss, they can strike as either white winged vultures picking a carcass or angels encircling a site of mourning. After the wins their arrival is delayed by lingering, celebratory crowds that are reluctant to leave.

We'd hardly acclimated ourselves before various Cardinals began spraying balls throughout the bleachers. Then Mark McGwire stood in. Even from more than a hundred yards away he was recognizable to the naked eye; tall and red-headed. Players jump in and out of the batting cage in bursts of a few swings at a time, taking frequent turns with teammates. McGwire's first cut launched one that I knew immediately was bound straight for me. An instant after it started its climb high into the sky came the resounding crack that confirmed the collision of the ball and McGwire's bat.

I was at once terrified and exhilarated about what was going to happen. It was a little like going undressed with intent for the first time except that my kids were with me and watching my every move.

But I had McGwire played perfectly and no moves were required. The closer the ball came the more obvious it was that I was its target. In those several seconds of the ball's flight I felt an almost personal relationship establish between me and the prodigious slugger at the plate. It was as though he'd deliberately aimed one my way as soon as he spotted me at my post; a "called shot" just for me.

I was standing in a walkway at the back of the section, just in front of the chain link fence that ends the ballpark in an area favored by the forward observers of the regular ballhawks on the street outside. Immediately in front of me was a steel railing running behind a row of seats, painted red long enough ago that some spots had chipped off. It was about belt-high, just like the pitch that had been detoured in my direction.

The ball's descent began and it was still right on course. I readied my glove. The boys were somewhere to my right and below me. The seats closest to me, the ones in front of the railing, were occupied by a family of four that included two kids younger than Max and Ben; a boy and a girl. They all wore Cardinal gear. My counterpart among them was busy snapping photos.

Here it came. I bent over the railing. The bleacher equivalent of a shoestring catch was called for. Still the ball had flown almost 400 feet on a parabolic tether between me and the game's greatest slugger du jour. It was mine; I had it all the way.

Except that I wasn't so limber as I used to be. I'd lost a step, even when no steps were required. I reached as low as I could, starting now to feel that some bluff I'd run but forgotten was being called.

Then the ball arrived. We touched. But instead of nestling into the pocket of my mitt where it belonged; where it had been addressed, the damn thing glanced off the tip of the webbing and began rattling between the seats in front of me just below the railing that had prevented me from better positioning myself for the catch.

The little girl had merely to reach down and pluck the ball off the concrete where it now lay motionless. She didn't even have a mitt.

She was relatively unimpressed but her brother and father both demonstrated a more appropriate level of appreciation.

It was an Old Man and the Sea-ish moment. I was supposed to catch a ball struck by *The Great McGwire*. Instead it flopped into the boat of a little girl who wasn't even fishing.

Max and Ben were not above letting me know they were disappointed in me. I was crestfallen, but didn't want them to know that. I was left to plead that if the play had occurred in a game it would not have been scored an error. To make the catch would have required a mildly exceptional play. I sounded like a prima donna with a lame alibi.

My self-defense ignored the old axiom that, "if you can touch it you can catch it." That was the standard applied by my two official scorers whose ruling was emphatic and unanimous: E-Dad...

There was a big league baseball game later that day at that same place [won by the Cubs, 4-3 in 10 innings] and it did provide our family with both consolation and redemption.

Rondell White was the Cubs' left-fielder. It is more or less customary at Wrigley Field that when whomever's manning that position finishes warming up between innings he tosses a ball into the seats parallel with the 3rd baseline, the family section of the left-field bleachers [*RIGHT HERE RONDELL!*] and the rowdier left-center bleachers on a rotating basis. Each area has three chances at a souvenir during the course of a regulation nine-inning game.

Just before the top of the 8th began, Rondell pegged his warm-up ball at us teetotalers for the third and final time. Ben reached up and made the play that his father, the aging veteran Santiago, had been unable to earlier.

The ball is a handheld, craterless moon. OFFICIAL MAJOR LEAGUE BASEBALL is stamped just above the facsimile signature of Allan H. Selig - COMMISSIONER. Below that, just across the red stitching of the seams, the word PRACTICE arcs in faint black stencil above the MLB logo. Above it, on the other side the seams, is the cursive Rawlings logo. On the other side of the ball - the bright side of the moon, if you will - in the spot reserved for autographing the ball now reads 6-7-01 in a handwritten black Sharpie font.

All-Starry Nights

About the time Chris and I were married my nephew, Christopher, and one of his high school baseball teammates, Eric, were both part-time employees at the pub that our family owned and operated. They were in their early 20's. Christopher was about to join the Marines and Eric was a recent graduate of Iowa State. During his college days he had another part-time job as an umpire.

By the time Max was born in July of 1991, Eric had a post-graduate degree from an umpire's school in Florida and both he and Christopher were bent on careers as men in blue; Eric at ballgames as an ump and my nephew on the streets of Des Moines as a cop.

I've written elsewhere of the circumstances of Max's birth but I am obliged to reset that scene at least this once more in light of where this particular story goes.

On the evening of July 9, 1991 I was alone in our living room watching baseball's All-Star game. Chris was elsewhere in the house enduring the late innings of gestation. She wasn't due for another couple of weeks.

Not long after the Cubs' Andre Dawson had homered off of Roger Clemens, Chris interrupted my regularly scheduled program-ming with this bit of [water] breaking news: *"M-I-I-I-K-E!!!"*

It was time for me to come in from the parental bullpen.

I offered Chris what relief I could en route to the hospital, which is to say none at all, but once we got there and were set up in a delivery room everything I learned at our Lamaze classes kicked right in.

"Hee-hee-hee-hoooo..." I demonstrated the prescribed breathing rhythm as the contractions squeezed a life out of her. I sounded like somebody on Quaaludes laughing hysterically.

Chris wasn't laughing. She wasn't hysterical either. She was la-boring. Real labor. The sort of labor compared to which hard la-bor and manual labor are Swedish massage.

In the middle of that night I finally met Max face to face. Wow!

What a first impression. Way to go, Chris! I knew *we* could do it.

It was July 10 by that hour. It was also Andre Dawson's birthday. Andre Dawson, the MVP of the National League in 1987, his first year with the Cubs. Andre Dawson, who was born and graduated from high school in the same years I did those two things. Andre Dawson, who knocked my wife into childbirth the night before with that blast off of Roger Clemens.

It was obvious. You didn't have to be a palm reader to see that our son was destined for the big leagues.

By the time Max's golden birthday hove into view up ahead, Eric had umped his way to the top. After doing his first big league games as a temporary substitute in 1996, he'd been hired as a regular, full-time major leaguer in 1999. Stars were aligning. The 2001 All-Star game was awarded to Seattle and set for July 10 of that year. Early in the 2000 season Eric called from the road to see if I'd be interested in tickets to that year's game in Atlanta. No, I told him, but for future reference, a couple for the '01 exhibition would make a cool birthday present for Max.

When the time came, Eric came through. He arranged for two tickets. Upon our arrival in Seattle we were to claim them at the hotel where MLB would be headquartered for the three-day All-Star festival.

I put together an itinerary. Unfortunately, seven year-old Ben would have to stay behind as the temporary man of the house. Eric could only get us two tickets and besides, the costs for a trio would have been too much. The game tickets alone had a face

value of $110 apiece, plus airfare, room, board and - the biggie
- souvenirs! Ben's birthday tends to fall around the Super Bowl
every year, so maybe someday I'd make it up to him.

To save on travel costs we drove to Omaha and flew from there. I
awakened Max very early on the morning of Saturday, July 7, and
handed him a birthday card that said "Get up! We're going to the
All-Star game!"

Des Moines to Omaha. Omaha to Denver. Denver to Seattle, where
we were met at the airport by a friend of mine then living in the
Seattle area. Brian shuttled us to our downtown hotel where we
checked in, unpacked, caught our breath and plunged in.

Our guide took us to a nice restaurant for a relaxing dinner with a
view of Puget Sound. Brian would not be our companion for the
baseball events but he was an invaluable source of directions and
more general local knowledge. I'd once lived briefly in Kirkland,
a Seattle suburb on Lake Washington, but wasn't in the city itself
often enough to remember much that would be useful now.

After dinner we turned in and chattered away most of the two
hours we'd borrowed traveling westward. We outlined the next
day's agenda: get up early, have breakfast, head for the MLB
headquarters hotel a couple of blocks away to pick up our game
tickets and, once they were in hand, head for the All-Star Fanfest
down near the waterfront and Safeco Field, home of the Seattle
Mariners; the nearly new ballpark where the game would be
played on Tuesday night, Max's 10th birthday.

We had pamphlets full of schedules, descriptions and maps of all that the Fanfest had to offer. We charted a course through a day that promised to be equal parts treasure hunt and carnival.

Because there was no other crossing to tomorrow, we slipped finally into shallow slumbers of exhausted anticipation.

Downtown Seattle was thoroughly abuzz, even by its already caffeinated standards, with All-Star hoopla. Pedestrian congestion was more of an impediment than the short distance we walked to reach the hotel serving as the temporary center of baseball's universe.

Once in the lobby we escalatored to the mezzanine level and took our places in the first of many lines we'd be parts of throughout our stay. It was long but swift, like a deep river with a strong current. As we neared the keepers of the tickets I began to fret that there would be a mix-up. An infrequent traveler still mystified by the inner workings of such anachronisms as rotary telephones and TV, I started imagining all the ways something could go wrong with a will-call ticket pick-up arranged via computer over a period of months involving at least three parties in cities scattered across a vast continent. We were going to reach the front of the line, announce ourselves and be greeted with a response of: "*Who?*" followed by laughter, followed by impatient jostling and shoves, followed by us being trampled to death under the hooves of real VIP's and baseball glitterati - I just knew it!

"Here you go, Mr. Wellman. Enjoy the game."

I couldn't believe it. Section 335; Row 16; Seats 5-6; "View Level" [clearly a euphemism for nosebleed section, but who cared?]. The tickets were impressively, importantly big; 3" x 8". And they were graphically cool. In the foreground was a base runner in full sprint leaving behind him a wake of embossed silver stars. Next to the date of the game it said "RAIN CHECK." Huh?

On the back was explained the rain check policy. It said, in part, that, "Should the game not progress to or beyond a point of play constituting a regulation game under official baseball rule 4.10(c) after the holder has been admitted to the park, this RAIN CHECK with the coupon attached will admit the holder to the game when played."

There ain't no rain checks for the All-Star Game, even in a city as moist as Seattle - not when it's scheduled for Max's golden birthday halfway across America in a stadium with a retractable roof!

We went back down to the main lobby to contemplate our passports and people-watch.

Max was sporting a Seattle Mariners cap that Brian had given him in a "When in Rome..." spirit. Within minutes it bore the signatures of Steve Garvey and Jim Palmer. Palmer's a hall-of-famer. Garvey's the pretentious villain who was instrumental in denying the Cubs and their fans access to the 1984 World Series when he wore the hideous brown and yellow of the San Diego Padres. That I not only allowed Max to solicit Garvey's autograph, but in fact steered him in the direction of the Prince of Darkness is a very precise barometer of the extent to which my judgment was star-fogged.

We couldn't help but notice an argument going on at the front desk between the clerk there and an elderly man, presumably a guest at the hotel. The old guy was visibly upset about something;

quite animated and getting more so. Frustrated, he wheeled from the counter and strode off in a huff. As he whisked past us at a pace that was anything but geriatric I recognized him. It was none other than our fellow Iowan, Bob Feller; Nile Kinnick's old battery-mate. Given his reputation for trading on his baseball resume rather than obliging kids for free and the mood he seemed in at the time, we decided it best to give him an intentional pass.

The same summer he graduated from high school Feller tied the major league single game strikeout record then held by Dizzy Dean. In 1940, when he was 21, Bullet Bob threw a no-hitter on Opening Day against the Chicago White Sox. He was a once-in-a-generation pitching prodigy who arrived ahead of the times of mediocre millionaires. If he's bitter and belated in his attempts to cash in on his indisputable greatness, who's to blame him? Carlos Zambrano can afford to give it away. By the time he tossed a no-hitter in the big leagues he was an above average but erratic and tempestuous pitcher making exponentially more in one season than Bob Feller made in a career; one interrupted, not incidentally, by distinguished military service in WWII. The only way Zambrano will ever get into the Hall of Fame is through the turnstiles. Paid admission is far more within his means than induction.

Enough of the lobby who's-who; it was time to buzz even nearer the flame. We left the hotel and walked down through Pioneer Square to the organized fan festivities. Luckily the weather was not the sort Seattle's known for; this day featured the type baseball was meant to be played in; a fortunate thing for the two of us and the thousands of others who queued up outside the Stadium Exhibition Center for entrance into the Fanfest. We were early and the doors hadn't yet opened. Though stagnant in terms of movement, there was an anticipant energy coursing through the ranks. Max was freely sharing the news that he was there in celebration of his birthday, courtesy of this rumpled, Cub-capped, spent-looking old fellow gasping behind me here; my dad.

When finally the lined-up throng was released inside, the stampede was on. Led by John Hancock, the title sponsor of the gala, corporate America was out in force like so many hucksters beckoning the fans come to the myriad baseball sideshows. Mastercard, Nextel, Gillette, Radio Shack, Century 21, Adidas, etc., ad infinitum…I signed up for a credit card to get Ben an All-Star beach towel. We got a photo of Max as the cover boy for a faux issue of *Baseball Weekly*. He and I collaborated on a mock telecast of the ceremony in honor of Cal Ripken shattering Lou Gehrig's consecutive games played streak. Max's pitching velocity was clocked by a radar gun. We ate. In the souvenir store we ran into and chatted with the wife of Mike Hampton, one of the National League All-Star pitchers, then with the Houston Astros. We played baseball trivia. We ate some more. We entered ourselves in lots of contests. Max posed for a caricature. We rested. We rest roomed. We spent.

Having chewed us up pretty good the Fanfest spat us out late in the afternoon. We staggered [well, I did; Max probably pranced] next door to reconnoiter the ballpark. We weren't due inside the premises until the following day when we'd be attending the official All-Star Home Run Derby, but we wanted to get a sense of the place. Safeco Field opened in 1999 and I'd actually attended one game there with Brian during its inaugural season. Max wanted in, but he'd have to wait. After a strolled orbit of the grounds I suggested we return to our temporary headquarters for some R&R. Max was ready to walk back the way we'd come that morning.

Instead his pack mule hailed a cab.

The best-laid plans of lucky men sometimes go even better than they could have imagined.

By the time our two intrepid tourists arrived the next day at the appointed site's base camp we were already taking on the customs of our surroundings. It was in that spirit that our first objective was to locate our seats in the "VIEW" level. We set upon a well-marked, concrete hiking trail that would lead us there. Upon our arrival at the stadium's summit we paused to take it all in. I especially was anxious for a crack at a deep breath. The "VIEW" of the baseball diamond far below was only familiar because we were such savvy baseballeers. A neophyte might have mistakenly thought the seats were beyond the range of meaningful observation of any activity staged on the faintly beige and green floor at the bottom of the huge bowl, but we were rather in awe. And that was before we realized the panoramic field of vision ranged all the way from the Seattle skyline to the waters of Puget Sound and the distant peak of Mt. Rainier. "VIEW" indeed!

Early enough so that our section was relatively vacant, I felt secure leaving Max alone in our seats with a pair of binoculars while I fetched some refreshment.

There I was, strolling the concourse of the upper reaches, scanning ahead for a concession stand. Here he came, walking briskly the other way, flanked by a couple of security wingmen. I think we may have exchanged that almost imperceptible nod that men reserve for one another. I was a few paces past him when the realization registered that he was Cal Ripken Jr. What was he doing in the "VIEW" level? I hit the brakes, wheeled around and gave pursuit. Just as I came up from behind he turned a corner and disappeared into a private hospitality suite that had been contrived under the auspices of Century 21 for the benefit of some of their top people. Oh, to be a top person.

Ripken was in the midst of what he'd announced would be the last year of his remarkable career. He was on a farewell tour through the American League during that 2001 season and would be playing the next evening in his 19th and final All-Star game. And our eyes had just met. And my birthday-celebrating son was sitting obliviously up in the stands looking down at the other all-stars through a pair of binoculars like bugs at the bottom of a canyon. I had to do something, but what?

I asked the security manning the entrance to the suite if Ripken would be there long. They were deliberately vague. Taking the chance that he would be signing and pressing the flesh for at least a short while, I ran back to our seats to grab Max. Once I had him in tow, we made sure that Ripken was still at the party, then raced down the concourse until we came to a souvenir shop. I dashed in and bought an official All-Star baseball. Thus equipped, we parked ourselves back outside the Century 21 shindig and waited.

It wasn't long before baseball's new Ironman emerged. He had a reputation for being patient with crowds of adoring fans, staying after games as long as it took to sign every ball, every cap, every mitt. But now, as Max approached with ball in hand, he brushed past him, seemingly in a hurry despite that his presence there was still largely undiscovered by most of the relatively few folks who were up there without being guests at the party.

I was aghast at the prospect that our ships might pass this close without colliding so I grabbed the wheel. I took the ball from Max and went again in pursuit of the street-clothed, steely-eyed, Baltimore Oriole.

I caught him when he paused to wait for a VIP elevator. Breathlessly I laid out our case; the birthday, the long trip, blah, waa, blah…I wasn't going to take no for an answer. Ripken said nothing. The elevator doors opened. He stepped into the car with his back to me. He turned and faced me. Just before the doors met each other halfway he reached out and accepted the ball and pen extended beseechingly toward him. He scrawled his name neatly on the sweet spot and gave the items back. The doors closed and he was gone; never said a word.

By then a small crowd had gathered. We made our way through it; the only ones carrying proof of our close encounter with a very rare bird; the Baltimore Superstar.

Ripken was the kind of ballplayer with appeal that crossed generational lines. Not only did he play every game for some 17 straight seasons, he was a throwback in the sense that he played his entire career with the same team, the one he grew up around while his dad was an Orioles coach and manager. In the days before free agency granted ballplayers the same rights to shop their services to the highest bidder that most American workers take for granted, players were essentially indentured to the team that first discovered and signed them to a professional contract. If there was little in that arrangement for the players, the fans at least were afforded the chance to bond with their favorites over the course of whole careers.

I passed the rest of our grand expedition taken by a spirit of the great warrior returning from a crusade with trophies and plunder for the tribe. I'm not sure how I got there from my obsequious performance in the presence of the mighty Ripken. The story grew even larger before it was ever told at home when Ripken belted a home run in the game on Tuesday night and was named the Most Valuable Player.

Some years later, when he was in middle school, Max made the ball into a desk lamp in shop class. It still works.

Time Out

Fathers and sons should collaborate on low-level conspiracies now and then. It is a bonding mechanism that can deepen a relationship and set it apart from the web of others that make up their separate lives. Not that you should establish a pattern of shared secrets that are kept from mothers/wives/sisters/daughters; just that it's okay for casual brotherhoods [and sisterhoods] to exist within the family framework like different rooms inside a house.

But you better be careful how you go about them.

I'm not sure if it was Mother's Day or Chris' birthday the year I enlisted Max and Ben in a spontaneous and ill-conceived plot of affection.

I pulled into the driveway and there they were, playing in the picket fenced front yard. They couldn't have been older than six and three because there was no Emma. Chris may have been pregnant with her. She was still inside her mother who was inside the house.

I was taken by a sudden impulse to snatch the boys and sneak the several blocks to our neighborhood grocery for some flowers and balloons in observance of whichever was the occasion.

We weren't gone even ten minutes. I was in a hurry to get back home and reap our just appreciation.

Boy, was I surprised when we returned to find Chris out in the yard frantically searching through a thicket of purple hysteria that clashed with the colorful bouquets we were clutching.

I'm not sure that she was ever before or has ever since been as angry at me.

It was as if the possibility that the boys had sneaked off with their romantic, mischievous father to arrange a sweet and special surprise for their mother hadn't even occurred to her. Perhaps if there had been some precedent. In lieu of one she immediately assumed the worst and we reappeared just in time to head off the issuance of an APB. Had there been a weapon at her disposal I would have been shot on sight.

So much for spontaneity.

Hero Worship

On January 12, 2002, we were back fanfesting again. This time around the Iowa Cubs brought in Bob Gibson and Billy Williams as the big name autographers. The boys' tickets cost five bucks apiece. Mine was $20. I can't remember how I purchased them but it must have been either online or over the phone because the name *WELLMAN* is printed on them, just above the word *CHILD* on Max and Ben's tickets; just above the word *ADULT* on mine. Besides the tickets we held you could hardly tell us apart.

I kept going on about the greatness and significance of Gibson, when he pitched for the Cardinals, and Williams, when he played left-field for the Cubs. Both played their way into in the Hall of Fame and the primes of their careers coincided with the prime of my boyhood.

Without realizing it I fell into the throes of a regression. There I was on E-bay in the days leading up to the event searching for Gibson and Williams baseball cards. At the fanfest I sent Max and Ben through the long line to get the cards signed as though I'd taken them to the bank to buy savings bonds.

Never a shrewd investor or dealmaker, I was haphazardly merging my nostalgia about baseball with some vague sense of a booming memorabilia market. I was trying to legitimize at a pragmatic level an inherently emotional, sentimental part of my life. Maybe I thought I could somehow recoup the lost treasure of baseball cards I'd collected and hoarded as a youngster only to have them vanish as I grew along with innocence, belief in Santa Claus and other riches from my childish portfolio. If so, I was anything but alone, for it was baby boomers like me that were driving the memorabilia craze.

Rarity may be a reasonable index of value, but there is something pathetic about grownups trading in bubblegum cards. It's there in the pretty sadness of my small pile of autographed cardboard portraits. I don't know if it matters that the signatures were acquired in person. When I've encountered Ernie Banks and Ron Santo on visits to Wrigley Field and gotten their signatures on items ranging from balls to cards to gloves to caps it's almost as though they've been notarizing my childhood.

Gee, when I put it that way…

Six weeks later Chris took me to Stephens Auditorium in Ames, the same place where Max and I had seen and heard the St. Olaf Choir, to see Garrison Keillor do a live broadcast of, *A Prairie Home Companion*. The date was February 23, 2002, so I suppose the tickets were a birthday present. They cost us $45 apiece, but we were only five rows from the stage, much closer to the performers than I was generally able to arrange at sporting venues.

Keillor is a rare combination of smart and funny. Baseball, on the other hand [at least as the Cubs go about it], is a strange brew of tears with a splash of cheers.

Popeye's Legs

E arly in May of 2002 a young pitcher by the name of Mark Prior arrived in Des Moines on the wings of hyperbole.

He'd been drafted by the Cubs a year earlier out of the University of Southern California. Prior was widely acclaimed as the finest amateur pitching prospect in the land at the time; some said he might be the best college pitcher ever.

His rapid shinny up the slippery pole of professional baseball sent him from Tennessee to Iowa that spring on his way to Chicago and seemingly inevitable major league stardom.

My two apprentices and I were in our choice seats behind the plate early on Tuesday, May 7, eager to see if the kid could possibly live up to the hype that preceded him.

He could.

In the first inning he struck out the side on 10 pitches. The umpire arbitrarily called one pitch a ball to justify his presence there on the field.

Prior fanned a total of 10 in seven innings, toying with most of the hitters as a cat would with mice caught in the trap of the batter's box.

That's what the swollen crowd had come expecting to see. He needn't have added the flourish of two home runs as a batter, but he did anyway.

It was a dazzling exhibition that further hastened his big league debut which he made a couple of weeks later against the Pittsburgh Pirates at Wrigley Field.

Strangely, the most striking physical feature of the prodigy with the golden arm was his legs. His calves were as disproportionate to the rest of him as were Popeye's forearms to his otherwise scrawny [sans spinach] frame.

He was what he was and that's all what he was. But that memorable night in Des Moines, he was somehow even more than we'd hoped for. We hadn't seen the last of him.

Best Play I Ever Made

I was alone again in Chicago on Wednesday, July 24, 2002.

I may have been in self-imposed quarantine after some unusually intense exposure to extended family. There'd been a reunion of Hillestads [my mother's maiden name from the old country - Norway] over the Fourth of July at Breezy Point, a lakeside resort near Brainerd, Minnesota. The event was coined, Uff-Da II. It was the sequel to Uff-Da I, held almost 40 years prior.

STUBS

Guess we just can't get enough of each other.

Keillor would have fit right in. There were lots of above average children, all of them Lutherans.

We had a softball game which was great fun and served to demonstrate that games with balls did not originate in Scandinavia.

Some of us skied on the water. Others did what they could.

Cousin Craig towed cousin Hans and me about the lake in a tandem slalom while we clung desperately to the outsized inner tubes that were the buffer between us and the surface of the lake, made hard by the speed and sharp angles that Craig steered. We bounced along like skipping stones.

I hadn't been that close to Hans since he was a toddler and I was a little leaguer and our family visited his while his father, Jim Hillestad - my uncle; mom's only brother - was teaching history at the University of Wisconsin-Oshkosh.

The tubing voyage resulted in a shoulder that felt dislocated when I tried to loosen up for the golf outing on the next day's agenda.

There were great stories around the fire pit after great meals in the evenings. The best one follows: When Uncle Jim decided to visit the land of the ancestors as a young man fresh out of college, the old home folks on the isle of Halsnoy off the rugged North Sea coast of Norway delegated the only member of their ranks who spoke any English whatsoever to meet and greet him. When Jim strode off the dock there was a hand sticking out of a wide grin eager to pull him to the family's bosom.

"Welcome, dumb bastard!"

You couldn't say it any friendlier.

The hand I was looking to shake later that July back at Wrigley Field was that of Ron Santo. Santo was a heel-clicking third baseman for the Cubs when I was a boy. Now he has no heels to click, having lost both of his lower legs to diabetes. Still, he remains a great ambassador for baseball in general and the Cubs in particular through his role as one of the team's radio broadcasters.

I'd brought along an old Wilson "Ball Hawk" mitt, model # 2184 with a facsimile signature of Ron Santo running up the inside of the pinkie, from my little league days. I hoped to get Santo to sign it for real. From all my visits to Wrigley Field over the years I knew where to find him if I got to the park early enough.

I was waiting when he drove up and parked in a lot reserved for media types. The lot is cordoned off by security staff, but as Santo made his way through it to the door that led to the Cubs' administrative offices he was fair game over a stretch of maybe 50 yards of sidewalk.

He seems to enjoy being recognized and appreciated by fans of all ages. I've never seen him be anything but affable. I told him how my dad and I used to listen on the radio when he was in his prime and asked would he please sign the glove I used back then. He was happy to oblige, signing along the outside of the thumb, and I thanked him before heading toward Waveland Avenue with the old glove on my left hand feeling suddenly restored. I even felt a bit rejuvenated myself and pounded the pocket a few times with my right fist.

When I joined the other ballhawks after stopping for a guzzle from the fire hydrant that the crew of Engine 78 [the firehouse on Waveland right across from Wrigley Field] always open like a drinking fountain during summer homestands, I felt less over-matched than usual. I'd never really come close to snagging a bat-ting practice clout, but maybe this would be my day.

The Cubs' opponent was the Philadelphia Phillies and they were taking their BP when I arrived on the scene. I positioned myself at the corner of Waveland and Kenmore and craned my neck to the skies looking for baseballs hurtling earthward like meteorites.

Nothing.

My neck started to get sore and I was losing interest. My mind wandered to the rooftop of the building on the northwest corner of the intersection, the one where a ball hit by Glenallen Hill once landed during a game I'd been watching on TV a few years back. What a blast! Over the left-field wall, over the bleachers, clear across Waveland, on top of a building several stories high on the far side of the street!

A little ways down Kenmore were faint remnants of spray paint commemorating prodigious home runs hit in years past by Dave Kingman and Sammy Sosa. I reflected on the cosmic significance of the facts that I grew up on a street called Kingman Boulevard and played golf on a municipal course named Waveland.

Abruptly I came out of my trance at the staccato scuffling of shoes on pavement. It was like a gang of fishermen angling for the same fish. But where was it? I looked up. Then I checked the flow of the ballhawks. I moved left with the pack. I saw the ball just as it crash landed in the middle of the street and ricocheted high toward the tree on the northeast corner. Like a racehorse with clear sailing along the rail I darted unimpeded toward the tree and could see that I was taking a good line. I thrust my gloved hand into a thicket of small branches and hoped.

I felt the ball nestle in the webbing of my magic mitt like a kid jumping into a snug bed.

Then followed an awkward moment or two of wondering what to do next. The veteran ballhawks with trunks full of BP homers picked them as routinely as apples from a tree. But this was my first one and it was long-awaited. It took a deliberate effort to appear nonchalant. One of my colleagues grudgingly mumbled, "nice grab."

I wondered who hit the ball. Logic dictated that it was probably a right-handed hitter with power since the Wrigley winds that day weren't blowing out toward the street. That narrowed the list of suspects to Mike Lieberthal, Pat Burrell and Scott Rolen. I decided it was Rolen on the basis that he, like Santo had been, was a slugger who also played great defense at third base.

After loitering several minutes more at the scene of my circus catch I ambled over to the nearest gate and entered the park where I could be alone with my prize; we made quite the couple - a 48 year-old boy and his crush stealing a few private moments in a nook of a crowded public space.

I called home, desperate for someone to share my great day with. The kids were scattered to summertime amusements. Chris was home alone. She did her best to sound suitably impressed and I did my best to sound more like her husband than one of her kids. The conversation that resulted was a little forced; sort of tentative and sheepish like ones between two people speaking different languages can be. We hung up and I looked at the red-stitched sphere tucked securely in the pocket of the leathery Wilson Ball Hawk, model # 2184 with both facsimile and authentic Ron Santo autographs and I realized the ball was not for me; it was the glove's. I brought them home. They've been together ever since.

From Shock & Awe to Shock & Shucks

In March of 2003 our whole family, except me, was on spring break.

Max was winding up his first year of middle school as a 6th grader and about to embark upon his last season of Little League.

Ben was a third-grade student and a promising southpaw.

I sometimes called them, The Bunkhouse Boys. As in, *"CUBS TAB BIG BEN WELLMAN - BUNKHOUSE BOYS EYE FLAG!"*

That was the mock headline I composed for a photo of the famous marquee at Wrigley Field. They put your faux message up there, snap a picture of it and send it to you for a few bucks. This one was framed and hung in Ben's bedroom; my answer on his behalf to the one in Max's room which read: *"PHENOM MAX WELLMAN INKS RECORD CUB PACT!"*

I enjoyed using sports page verbs like *TAB* and *INK* and *EYE* and sports page nouns like *PHENOM* and *PACT*.

This was also the year that *GREENWOOD SCHOOL TABS EMMA WELLMAN - KINDERGARTEN ROOKIE WOWS PROFS!*

Chris too was back in school, attending night classes to complete a teaching degree.

I was the prosperous innkeeper who rounded up the quintet for a trip to Arizona.

When the five of us traveled together the most frequent destination was Minnesota lake country for a week at the breast of Mother Nature. Once we'd gone to Florida between Christmas and New Year's, but the weather was subpar. This was our first visit to the Southwest and it was timed to coincide with spring training near Cub headquarters in Mesa.

We all attended a game at HoHoKam Park in Mesa on March 19. All I remember of it is that the weather was just the way it was supposed to be, the Cubs' opponents were the Anaheim Angels and His Majesty Sammy Sosa played a few innings, excused himself, showered and left the premises to great fanfare before the game had even ended.

The greater attraction for the kids on this trip was the swimming pool at our hotel. It was rather ordinary by the standards of hotel pools except that a plaster arch crossed over it like the handle on a basket. It was not in play at all, but enthralled them nonetheless.

While we were off in this other world the real one intruded. We were having dinner in a chain restaurant; verifying that fries and ketchup in Arizona rise to the standards we'd become accustomed to in Iowa, when President Bush appeared on the Big Brother sized TV screen to solemnly announce that he'd unleashed something called "Shock and Awe" upon Iraq. It sounded like the name of a Rolling Stones tour. Near the end of his remarks the furrows in his brow reassuringly vanished when he flashed that self-satisfied expression of his where the mouth spreads into a grin while the scalp somehow simultaneously pulls the forehead back. It's like your mom making the wrinkles in a bedspread disappear with a whoosh and a smoothing stroke of her hand.

I didn't know what to think at the time. I must admit to a certain measure of awe at the might of the American military and a definite level of respect for its personnel, especially those in the field of operations. And I wondered what it must be like to sit in on the sessions that lead to decisions as momentous as whether or not to go to war. Me, I sometimes grapple with the choices presented by vending machines.

In wars gone by baseball was as impacted as any other facet of American life. There's talk now of putting asterisks beside some of the most prodigious statistical achievements of modern players because they're thought to be inflated by use of steroids. There were players from the WWII and Korean War eras [Bob Feller and Ted Williams, most notably] whose resumes were deflated by military service.

With regard to the current War on Terror, brought to our shores late in the 2001 season and sharply escalated by President Bush during spring training of 2003, baseball's role has been to help maintain a reassuring sense of normalcy on the home front.

We at our house did our Yankee Doodle Dandy best as never before during that '03 season.

We returned home and the baseball season began with Rod Beck, the star relief pitcher for the Cubs during their run to the 1998 National League playoffs, living in his RV just beyond the center field fence at Principal Park in Des Moines. He was trying to pitch his way back to the big leagues and within a couple of months he did. But not until he hosted an episodic cocktail party with fans of the Iowa Cubs. He let it be known that after home games, if the neon martini glass in his window was on, the bar was open and folks were welcome to drop in for a beer. Many did. I was tempted, but didn't. I wanted to swap memories with him of that one-game playoff for the NL wildcard berth in '98, a game he saved by getting Joe Carter to pop-up to Mark Grace for the last out of the game.

But I was nine years sober by then and I had a hunch there was something rotten in Rod's RV. Played by the media generally as the sweet, folksy story of a millionaire ballplayer on his way out of the game that made him rich who hadn't forgotten where he'd come from, I detected a whiff of the carnival sideshow. For sure, had I still been drinking I would have worn out my welcome at Beck's place. Years before I'd gotten friendly enough with a past manager and pitching coach of the I-Cubs that we drank after hours at my pub until the janitor shooed us out at dawn when he came to sweep and mop the floors.

After one last successful fling in major league baseball Rod Beck was found dead at the age of 38 in the summer of 2007. He died alone at the hands of a drug that first addicted and then killed him. I never got physically closer to Rod Beck than you could get by buying a ticket to a ballgame. Still, I knew him pretty well.

But speaking again of Yankees, the ones from New York not only came to Wrigley Field that summer, they came over the first weekend after school let out.

All five of us made the trip to Chicago. Once we got there the itineraries got customized and complicated.

Friday, June 6 was travel day. We hit the road at dawn, plenty early to arrive in town, check in downtown and split up along gender lines for the afternoon recreations. The guys took the red line to Addison St. where we had upper deck box seats in section 433 on the first base side of the old dowager ballpark. From there you can see clear to Lake Michigan. The ladies got no further than the Magnificent Mile, conveniently juxtaposed within a short stroll of our weekend headquarters.

The Cubs were too generous as hosts on this day and lost 5-3 after Carlos Zambrano quickly pitched them into a 5-0 hole in the first three innings.

Corey Patterson hit his 12th homer of the year for the Cubs in the 8th, but it was too little too late.

Patterson was the young gazelle who'd passed through Des Moines on the fast track to stardom in the big leagues. After some growing pains he appeared to be in the midst of a breakout season. His batting average was comfortably above .300, and he was stealing bases and flagging down anything hit remotely near his post in center field. A star, it seemed, was in the making. Every time we saw him play now the boys would razz me about a pratfall he took in a game we watched on TV when he was a rookie. Patterson was at the plate and I mentioned his speed. I said how much I'd enjoy watching him leg out a triple and he lashed the next pitch down the line into the right field corner.

"There he goes!" I yelled, rising to my feet. "Watch him run like a deer!"

Just about then the fleet-footed Patterson was hanging a left turn at 2nd base in full throttle. He tripped over the bag and sprawled in the dirt where he was tagged out. The boys roared with laughter, not at Patterson, but at me - the jinx.

Later that summer of '03 Corey Patterson's one fine season was cut short by a knee injury. He'll never be as good again as he was that year.

Day Two of the Yankee series dawned bright and sunny. It was scheduled for a noon start to accommodate a national TV network.

Despite that Roger Clemens was slated to pitch for the Yanks in search of his 300th career win, a milestone previously reached by only 20 or so pitchers in baseball's long history, the boys opted to go shopping with Chris. Max had a nice baseball bobblehead doll collection that he wanted to add to through a memorabilia shop in Water Tower Place. Ben was weary of the Wrigley hustle and bustle from a day earlier. Besides, I had no tickets for the Saturday game. I'd been able to barge through the virtual queue in February and score five seats for the last game of the historic series [the Yankees' first visit to Wrigley since the World Series in 1932 that included Babe Ruth's famously alleged "called shot" home run] which would also be nationally televised on that Sunday evening. But it looked like I was on my own for the Saturday matinee.

I scrubbed up and left early for Wrigleyville since my first order of business was acquisition of a ticket for the game. It didn't take me long to acquire an aisle seat in Terrace Reserved Section 233, Row 13 on the Addison Street side of the ballpark [Wrigley's address is commonly cited as Clark & Addison. Addison runs parallel to the first baseline, Sheffield Ave. to the base path between first and second base, Waveland Ave. to the one that connects second and third, and Clark St. the homestretch of third to home]. I don't remember what I paid, probably a repression of a self-indulgent extravagance.

It was still early so I crossed the street and went into the convenience store at the corner of Addison & Sheffield to get a soda and a pack of smokes. While I stood in line at the checkout, a misty blue Jaguar pulled into the parking lot. Joe Borowski, incumbent Cubs' closer; the same job once held by Rod Beck, climbed out and came inside to buy several tins of chewing tobacco. It was like seeing a gunslinger at the general store buying bullets to be spat later during a shootout on the street in front of the townsfolk.

Borowski had paid some of his minor league dues in Des Moines so I was compelled to offer him a hearty, "Good luck Joe!" as a self-appointed delegate of Iowa's baseball fans.

After my impromptu pep talk with "Bobo," as I liked to call him, I meandered down Clark and posted myself along the chain link fence that keeps fans out of the parking lot where the Cub players park their cars. Even the mediocre journeymen can afford to wheel around town in expensive rides and the lot was full of them. Cadillac, Lexus and Mercedes play for every team in the league. BMW has become as much a part of the big leagues as RBI and ERA.

While I waited to spy a noteworthy Cub or two pulling up to work, droves of stadium workers began arriving to their jobs, walking from the bus stop on Clark or the "L" station on Addison. I overheard a conversation between a couple of vendors about the used car one of them had just bought; a street level, grass roots symposium on trickle down economics. The beermen and the cracker jackers are the small fry steering their lives off of the dorsal fins of big sharks. It may be a shame if the Cubs don't win, but a summer of packed houses at Clark & Addison is good for a lot of people besides the lavishly paid ballplayers.

I saw Kerry Wood arrive that day. He was to pitch for the Cubs, opposed by the legendary Clemens. I yelled something encouraging at him from across the parking lot like a little boy with some real part of his life riding on the outcome of this one in a summer long series of 162 ballgames.

In May of 1998, when Wood was a baby-faced rookie, he struck out 20 Houston Astros in only his fourth start in the big leagues to tie a record first set by Clemens. Now he stood between his boyhood idol and a career milestone. Such is the poetry of baseball.

There had been about 15,000 in attendance at Wrigley Field on that gray, dreary day five years prior to this one; Wood put more K's in the box score than there were in the stands [K being the symbol for strikeout chosen a long time ago by journalist Henry Chadwick who is generally credited with devising the system of shorthand by which notes are taken on a ballgame while it's in progress]. Today there were roughly 40,000.

One of them who passed me on the street outside the park appeared to be Uncle Sam. He looked like the Yankee logo come to life.

The whole neighborhood was abuzz. I'm sure I was smiling, though I was all by myself.

Early in the game Wood collided with his Korean first baseman, Hee Sop Choi, in pursuit of a pop fly. Choi went to the hospital in an ambulance, Wood went back to work and Eric Karros came in to play first base.

Later, in the bottom of the 7th, Karros blasted a three-run homer off the reliever brought in to protect Clemens' 1-0 lead and delirium reigned.

Bobo pitched the ninth inning to preserve the victory for Wood and the Cubs.

The stage was perfectly set for the third and rubber game the next night.

When the five of us arrived late the following afternoon to jockey for position outside the front gates it was raining - hard. Chris and I huddled beneath an overmatched umbrella like Alice and Ralph Kramden. We exchanged glances like matrimonial chess moves. Hers asked, "Is this really necessary?" Mine said,"Baby, you're the greatest."

I tried to pacify the kids with reminders that once the gates opened, the gatekeepers would be passing out free replicas of the style of cap worn by the Cubs when last they'd faced the Bronx Bombers decades ago, courtesy of the Heileman Brewing Company, makers of Old Style. Max and Ben were at least intrigued. Emma was unimpressed.

Our seats were in the familiar Family Section of the left field bleachers, but this seemed like a night when a spot in the grandstand under the cover of the upper deck might be a better vantage point.

The gates opened at last and we collected our free souvenir caps. By the time we made our way through the teeming concourse, climbed the short flight of concrete steps to our section and emerged in the relative intimacy of the temperate corner of the grounds a vivid rainbow was manifesting in the southeastern sky. Cheap, Cub-logoed ponchos, the rare utilitarian souvenir, were removed as widely as clothes at Woodstock and cast aside to quickly depreciate in the gathering muck underfoot.

Jim Belushi happened by and graciously posed for a photograph with yours truly, believed to be the only one in existence of the two of us together. The rainbow loomed radiantly in the background like an archway to be passed through on the road to triumph over the vaunted Yankees.

In the first inning Moises Alou put the Cubs ahead with a three-run rainbow of his own into the left-center bleachers.

Later in the game the mercurial Sosa lined the 2,000th hit of his career and was rewarded with yet another of the standing ovations he'd become accustomed to at his home park. This despite that he was in the lineup on bail pending a ruling on his appeal of a suspension for getting caught using a corked bat earlier in the week.

Performance enhancers were becoming so prevalent that even the equipment was on steroids. Gloves were getting as big as leather geisha fans.

Alou was given to urinating on his hands to toughen their skin against blisters, an organic and cheap alternative to batting gloves, but one I was reluctant to suggest to the boys on our annual pre-season shopping sprees for the latest gear at sporting goods stores.

The Cubs' other ballyhooed young pitcher, Mark Prior, would get the victory this night, striking out 10 Yanks to go with the 11 Wood had fanned the previous day, but not until Bobo picked a runner off of first base to finally end the New Yorkers' too little-too late rally. The 8-7 win capped off a rollicking weekend that us Cub fans especially wanted to believe was a World Series preview.

Time would tell.

It Might Be…It Could Be…It is!

B ack home Max was winding down his little league career.

He wasn't a natural ballplayer, yet baseball may have first revealed some of his strongest traits and assets.

For one thing, he's always been determined.

Prior to the '03 season he'd never hit much. He pitched some as an 11 year-old, but every time he seemed to be settling into a groove on the mound he'd uncork a pitch so far outside the lines that it made batters wonder if they were safe there in the batter's box.

He had a growth spurt prior to this last go 'round on the small diamond. It was the third and last season when we were coach and player as well as father and son.

As in the previous two seasons our team, the Cubs, lost approximately as much as we won. We played at the Triple A level in the Raccoon Valley pecking order; the less accomplished of the two tiers provided for the 10-12 year-olds. Many of Max's school buddies played in the Majors, a fact he'd accepted when he was 10 and 11 but was disappointed by this season because he thought he'd done well at the preseason tryouts and should have been drafted into the higher league. I told him they probably figured they'd lose a Triple A coach if he moved up so no one picked him.

The Majors had paid umps. In Triple A reluctant dads were conscripted into service behind the plate. Once when the count on a batter reached maybe 16 balls and 15 strikes I had to tell the poor guy on duty that the clicker he held and looked at after each pitch was manually operated; it didn't count balls and strikes by itself!

Max became a standout player. Even at this level it was a development I hadn't seen coming. Ben was smallish for his age but more naturally coordinated than his big brother. But he'd never sit still to watch a game with me on TV or listen to one on the radio; he'd rather go out and play/announce an imaginary one by himself in the front yard. Max, on the other hand, better understood a game he wasn't as well equipped to play.

That summer he threw harder than any other kid in his league. He was still what's sometimes known in the big leagues as "effectively wild." His velocity coupled with the chance that he might occasionally throw one off the backstop kept batters from digging in against him.

At the plate he thumped the ball as he never had before. Over the fence home runs were few and far between on the Triple A field but Max knocked several shots that bounced off the wall.

Two days after we returned from the Cubs-Yankees series in Chicago we played our next-to-last regular season game. Suddenly it happened. I was coaching first base when Max connected and sent one soaring to left-center. I watched it sail over the fence; a boundary that all kids long to cross. Then I nonchalantly bonked him on the helmet as he turned the corner towards second base and trotted the triumphant lap of the square back home where a clot of teammates formed and absorbed him.

It was the shot heard 'round our world.

A week or so later, in the last game Max would ever pitch, the first batter of the game lined out to left. The last 17 outs were strikeouts.

He went out on top. Mickey Mantle wished he could have said that.

We're Baaaack!

I n July we were back in Chicago again.

The Atlanta Braves were in town to take on the Cubs in a series that would lead into the midseason All-Star break. The All-Star game was being hosted that year by the crosstown White Sox at their relatively new ballpark on the south side.

STUBS

The usual trio of us had some nice Terrace Boxes for an afternoon game at Wrigley on Thursday, July 10, Max's birthday. We also had tickets for a couple of All-Star events on the 13th. One was the fanfest at McCormick place that morning. The other was an afternoon doubleheader consisting of an absurd celebrity softball spectacle and a more sensible "futures" game that featured rising American prospects versus young talent from around the world.

We couldn't afford admission to the main event of the All-Star festival, but the sideshows were within our means and would round out another long weekend in our baseball home away from home.

When me and the boys arrived at our seats in Section 237, Row 4 for Max's birthday party I noticed that the breeze, almost as significant a factor at Wrigley Field most days as the lineups, was blowing in our faces on the first base side of the "Friendly Confines." That meant it was coming in from left field and would act as a suppressant on fly balls struck in that general direction. I confidently announced to my proteges that, "we won't see any homers to left today - the wind's blowing in."

We stood for the anthem as the American flag atop the scoreboard and the subordinate team pennants arranged in order of the league standings beneath it flapped colorfully against the backdrop of the high blue sky.

Then we settled in. I'd only just cracked open my first peanut when the game's first batter, Atlanta shortstop Rafael Furcal - not exactly a power hitter - blasted a home run to guess where? The left field bleachers. Mr. Jinx strikes again. The boys got yet another kick out of my vast store of baseball wisdom and insight.

The Cubs were soundly beaten that day, 13-3. The Braves record at that point stood at 59-31. They were the frontrunners in the Eastern Division of the National League. The Cubs were sputtering along at 46-45, fortunate to be assigned to the so-so Central Division where they were only a couple games back in spite of themselves.

On Saturday we paid a visit to the Field Museum, a place where we'd previously gone and spent whole days gaping at reconstructed dinosaurs and well-pickled mummies. This time we were drawn by a particular and temporary exhibit called "Baseball as America." It was essentially a branch office of the Hall of Fame on display in Chicago and was highlighted by one of Babe Ruth's bats which appeared to have been hewn from a railroad tie. The glimpse at baseball's rich history was the perfect prelude to the guess at its future we would attend the following day.

Sunday presented some logistical challenges. We took a cab to the cavernous McCormick Place, on schedule to enter at 12:00 as specified on our tickets. The exhibition baseball and softball games were slated for 4:00 in another part of a big city.

I'm not sure when we left the fanfest, but we probably overstayed there like gluttons at an all-you-can-eat buffet. When we belatedly decided to head back to the hotel so we could drop off our lootings and catch the train to the ballpark the competition for cabs was stiffer than we'd planned for.

Max and Ben were oblivious to the time crunch we were under, but I was beginning to feel it. I hustled us in and out of the hotel and down to the Grand St. "L" station. We might just make it, but wait... I didn't have correct change for our train fares. The machine didn't vend money out, it just vacuumed it in and what human presence manned the depot was only there to give directional advice and offer turnstile instruction.

I had to make a mad dash back up to the street with the boys scrambling to keep up. I was at condition red on the stress-o-meter now as we jaywalked over to a drugstore to get change for a twenty. Sorry; no-can-do - you gotta buy something. I could have used some over-the-counter tranquilizers, but instead I grabbed a pack of gum, the better to gnash my teeth on, and we raced back to the train station. It was then that I thought out loud, forgetting for a moment the small entourage trailing at my heels.

"If I had to live in this town I'd be an axe murderer!" I opined; louder than I realized and much to the chagrin of my traveling companions and other pedestrians within earshot.

What followed was a quiet and crowded ride to the home of the White Sox; an excursion that felt like going behind enemy lines. By the time we got there I'd had sufficient time to decompress and recalibrate my mood to suit the occasion. In the years since it was first uttered, the axe murderer line has de-carbonated and been oft-quoted by Max in a lighter context, now a benign footnote in our family folklore.

None of us remembers much detail of the game we saw that showcased the next wave of big league stars, but they were there. Grady Sizemore was rising through the minor leagues then. He won the game's Most Valuable Player [MVP] award before becoming an all-star centerfielder for the Cleveland Indians. Ryan Howard also played on the American squad. He's since been named the MVP of the National League as a member of the Philadelphia Phillies.

The World team included future Cubs Angel Guzman and Felix Pie. Neither of them has yet fully materialized as a bona fide big leaguer, but my path would cross with both of them again at a much closer range.

Peaking for the Pennant Race

By Labor Day weekend the Cubs were still in the thick of the race in the Central Division. A crucial five-game series with the first-place Cardinals loomed at Wrigley. I felt that we, like a good newspaper, should be represented there, so I hit the road again. The roughly five hour trip east to Chicago was starting to become almost routine; a generally monotonous drive on Interstates 80 and 55 that's always highlighted by a breathtaking crossover of the Mississippi River that divides Iowa from Illinois.

I traveled on the morning of Saturday, August 30. The game that day vs. the Milwaukee Brewers was scheduled for a late 3:05 start in accommodation of national television. I figured the Cubs would warm up for the big Cardinal series by beating the Brewers a couple of times, but I was wrong. They lost Saturday and Sunday and limped into the pivotal showdown with their arch rivals from St. Louis.

Despite the long-standing rivalry between the teams, I've always respected the Cardinals. For one thing, they sport classy uniforms. I like the birds perched at either end of the bat emblazoned on the blouses. I like the pretzeled S,T & L on the crest of the caps. That logo reminds me of the plastic adapters that used to fit 45 rpm records securely on the spindle of turntables.

Another factor may be that I am used to seeing actual Cardinals where we live. Young bears are not so prevalent.

Monday, Labor Day, dawned forebodingly. The skies were full of huge gray water balloons and it wasn't long until they burst open. It was September 1 and the fates seemed to be conspiring against the Cubs as per tradition.

The game was scheduled for a 1:20 start but that came and went with no change in weather conditions. The game simply had to be played, come hell or high water, the latter prospect a very real one. A doubleheader was already on tap for the following day that included a makeup of a game rained out earlier in the season. The pitching staffs in particular would have been unduly taxed by doubleheaders on consecutive days.

Everybody waited.

My problem was that I had to get back to Des Moines and I didn't like driving at night. I figured if I left Chicago by 4:00 or so I'd be on the outskirts by dusk if I drove @ 75 MPH and made just one combo pit stop to fill the car's bladder and empty mine. I decided to wait as long as I could in hopes of seeing as much of the game as I could.

Rain delays at any ballpark are no fun, but at Wrigley Field they are particularly tedious - for all the right reasons. For all its charm when a full slate of major league baseball is underway in midsummer, the gigantic scoreboard is ill-equipped to entertain in the event of bad weather. It features no Jumbotron and I prefer it that way. I am also glad the Cubs have no silly-suited mascot strutting the dugout roofs like they were a vaudevillian stage. The game is the thing. On occasions when that's been delayed at its outset or interrupted in progress one is left to take shelter in the seats overhung by the upper deck or huddle in the overcrowded concourse beneath; there to suffer the company and scents of the other patrons.

What creature comfort is to be found at this place is linked thoroughly and for better or worse to Mother Nature. Depending on the severity of your Cub neurosis, tranquility may be contingent on the fortunes of an almost equally irresistible force - the Cubs.

I had driven my car north from downtown that morning to enable a quick getaway whenever the time came to head for home. My arrival in Wrigleyville was so early that I was able to park on the street in front of the police precinct house a few blocks east of the ballpark on Addison [not to get too futuristic, but some sweet, riotous day that is somehow both unimaginable and inevitable, Wrigley Field's location smack between a police station and a firehouse is going to pay public safety dividends].

As 4:00 approached and the field was still covered with the massive blue tarpaulin raincoat I gave up and left. I'd been at the ballpark for almost seven hours and had to go before a pitch was thrown. Under a cloud of resigned self-pity as dark as the ones stalled overhead I steered the car to Lakeshore Drive and started out of town. I was soggy and tired and not looking forward to the next 350 miles.

About the time I looped off of Interstate 55 onto Interstate 80 and pointed west, the radio reported that the tarp was coming off and the procrastinated ballgame was finally about to begin. It was like picking up Pat Hughes and good ol' Santo hitchhiking. At least I'd have some company for the rest of the trip, but I was not optimistic about the Cubs' chances, given the dispiriting weekend I'd just endured.

At least Prior was pitching for the Cubs. He'd been practically a sure thing coming down the stretch and might be just the tonic the team needed to set the tone for the week ahead.

A pitchers' duel ensued with Prior's counterpart, the veteran Woody Williams, matching him goose egg for goose egg through the first four innings. As I was crossing the Mississippi back into Iowa - rounding second as it were - the Cubs started slapping Williams around to the tune of a five-spot in the bottom of the 5th. Prior made sure it was more than enough, lasting eight innings as the Cubs won the opening round of a five-round bout, 7-0.

Tuesday's twin bill was split, a game apiece, but the Cubs won the next two in dramatic fashion by scores of 8-7 [coming back from a 6-0 deficit] and 7-6. They'd started the pivotal series 2.5 games behind the Cardinals in 3rd place. After taking four out of five they'd passed them and were off and running to their best month of the long season. When the Cardinals left town on Thursday night with their tail feathers plucked, they were the 3rd place team. The Cubs were running 2nd, half a game behind the Houston Astros, but they suddenly had the look and feel of the team to beat.

When I'd moped out of Wrigley Field late on Labor Day afternoon I was weighed down by wet clothes and the familiar hunch that the season was all but over. It turned out that the Cubs weren't done yet and neither was I.

Clinch Mobs & Lucky Numbers

Earlier in the year the Cubs had announced plans to retire Ron Santo's jersey #10 on Sunday, September 28, 2003. Immediately I logged onto their ticketing system to see what I could scrounge, but by then only single seats remained and they were scattered around the park. I got a nice Terrace Box seat on the aisle in Section 236; Row 3. When I discovered the same seat was available for the Saturday game and that the game was scheduled for the 3:00 start time that made game day car travel from Des Moines easier, I grabbed it too; might as well kill two games with one trip.

If the Labor Day weekend had been a disappointing one, my next visit was probably the most glorious I've ever made to Wrigley Field.

When I left home on the 27th the Cubs' magic number for clinching the Central Division pennant was three. Magic numbers are a mystical part of the calculus of baseball that Cub fans don't often need to bother with. They derive from a formula that incorporates the number of games remaining and the number of games separating one team from another in the standings.

The Cubs had been on a September tear that started on that soggy Labor Day against the Cardinals. At the start of play on the 27th their record was 86-73. The Astros were a half game behind them at 86-74. Accordingly, any combination of Astro losses and Cub victories totaling three would clinch the pennant for the Cubs.

It was possible that number could be achieved that day. The Astros were hosting the Milwaukee Brewers in Houston and the Cubs had a doubleheader at home vs. the Pirates. I knew what I was hoping for but had no idea what to expect.

Prior was pitching the first game for the Cubs that day and he'd won nine out of 10 down the stretch so I liked our chances in the opener. I actually arrived just in time. The doubleheader was not originally scheduled; it resulted from a rainout of Friday's game. Consequently, the schedule calling for a single game at 3:00 was revised. The first game of the day began at 1:20. The sky was ashen but dry.

It was scoreless for three innings before the Cubs took control with two runs in both the 4th and 5th innings.

As the game progressed people's attentions divided between the action on the field and the numbers being manually posted on the scoreboard that charted the course of the game going on in

Houston. The Astros had jumped in front with a run in the bottom of the 1st, but the Brewers took the lead with a deuce in the top of the 3rd. When a big white '3' slid into the compartment reserved for the top of the 6th and alerted the crowd that the Astros were now losing 5-1 an ovation erupted that was incongruous to the game we were all actually watching.

The hell with texting; this was good news spreading the old-fashioned way.

By the time Bobo Borowski got the last out of the Cubs' 4-2 triumph everyone knew that the Astros had lost. If the Cubs could win the nightcap and sweep the doubleheader the magic number countdown would reach zero and Wrigley Field would rocket into orbit.

The intermission between games was tingly. I phoned home to set the stage for what might be in the offing and to make sure I'd have an audience on standby for eyewitness accounts during the second game.

Game two got started a little after 5:00. In the bottom of the first Sosa recharged the crowd with a prodigious home run deep into the center field bleachers. When the Cubs added five more runs in the 2nd the Pirates were reduced to extras in a play that now was headed toward a foregone conclusion. The mood in the stands was marvelously free of tension. The last seven innings were a formality which we happy 40,000 passed in a collective giggle like there was helium in the atmosphere.

After the Cubs turned a double play to end the game and officially become Central Division champions I called home and just let the boys listen to the din over which I could not be heard.

It occurred to me that now the retirement of Santo's #10 the next day could be more thoroughly joyous. Had the pennant race not been resolved in the Cubs' favor there would have been an inhibiting subtext at work like a mute on a trumpet. Santo himself would have been a subdued guest of honor at his own bash - he was as much a Cub fan as anyone in the ballpark on any given day.

All that remained to wish for was good weather.

I arose on Sunday morning to the same bland, colorless sky of the day before. It was an institutional shade. Rain felt probable.

I walked several blocks to St. James, an Episcopal cathedral downtown. There was a plaque in the lobby denoting that Abraham Lincoln had worshipped there after being nominated for the presidency in 1860. I was duly impressed at the time. I was also in a mood for thanksgiving, but not because the Cubs were a big step closer to the promised land. So help me you-know-who, they don't even draw mention in my prayers unless it's deliverance I'm seeking. No, I was simply feeling blessed to be who and where I was. Ironically I was the same guy who'd marauded through these same streets many times in what was now recalled as almost another lifetime. There'd been many road trips to Chicago when I was out of my element and out of my mind. To have been there on occasions such as the two that drew me there on this particular weekend might have been the death of me. Instead I was living as never before.

They were handing out commemorative Santo baseball cards at the gate. I took mine and went to my seat where I purchased a hot dog and a soda and proceeded to review Santo's illustrious career as it was statistically detailed on the back of the card.

Somehow he was credited with a league-leading 164 games played in 1965 even though the schedule only called for 162 [there were two "ties" credited to the Cub ledger that year, one of them on Opening Day. Both games were played at Wrigley Field and had to be stopped as sundown approached - just like we had to in the sandlot days of childhood. Later such games would be declared suspended and re-sumed on another day at the point of interruption, but in '65 they were replayed entirely and the players' stats were entered into the official record]. In 1964 he led the league in triples with 13; a rare accomplishment for a player not known as a speed merchant. Four times he led the league in walks. Not mentioned was the fact that all of his statistics were compiled despite that he was an insulin-depen-dent diabetic throughout his playing days.

Gradually a ceremony was being prepared on the area of the play-ing field between home plate and the pitcher's mound. Microphones and chairs and dignitaries appeared. Everything was in place ex-cept weather befitting the occasion. It remained bleak until just about the time all the introductory speakers finished extolling the many merits of Santo and it was his turn at the mike.

While he thanked the fans and his ex-teammates and told the crowd that having his number retired by the Cubs to fly forever above Wrigley Field meant more to him than enshrinement at Cooperstown [a truth at that moment that is otherwise probably false] the emotion rising off of the place stirred into the gray sky, opening a patch of blue and kicking up enough of a breeze to unfurl the #10 flag being raised on the left field foul pole to hang below Ernie Banks' #14. Opposite them on the right field pole was Billy Williams' #26. Those three were the heart of the Cubs' line-up throughout my boyhood and I pledged my allegiance to them many times. I may have done it again that day. There were people all around me with tears in their eyes while Santo spoke but he wiped them away when he concluded his remarks with a rousing pep talk about the upcoming playoff series with the Braves.

The regular season finale, already rendered moot in terms of the divisional pennant race the Cubs had won the previous day, now had another tough act to follow. Rather than stay to watch a makeshift lineup go through the motions of a meaningless game while most of the champagne-soaked regulars took the day off I decided to get an early start for home.

Never had I attended as many Cub games in a season as I did in 2003. I resolved to come back for more.

The Ivy in Autumn

A s soon as I got home from the last series of the regular season I began scouring the internet for tickets to playoff games. By the time the Cubs finished off the Braves in the first round [the same team that swept them out of the '98 post-season] I had made arrangements for single tickets to the first two games of the National League Championship Series [NLCS] at Wrigley

Field. The Cubs were facing the Florida Marlins, a team in existence for barely a decade that had nevertheless already won a World Series crown.

I bought both tickets on E-bay. By then I'd thrown common sense to the wind and people were starting to notice the change in me as I transformed from a lifelong Cub fan to an out-and-out groupie.

My nails grew long and claw-like. Suddenly I craved honey on my peanut butter sandwiches. I was not only wearing my Cub hat to church, I refused to take it off during services. Cub decals were plastered on all of our stuff. I started passing them out to strangers like a street corner Harry Caray Krishna.

The face value of the tickets was $50 for game one [Terrace Reserved] and $70 for game two [Field Box]. I paid considerably more for each, a total in the neighborhood of $500. Not only that; I left for Chicago with neither ticket in hand.

Game one's was secured via rendezvous with the seller beneath the Wrigley marquee on game day. We found each other based on wardrobe descriptions. The whole transaction smacked of espionage ["I'll be wearing a sign around my neck that says 'Cub Dork' - code name: 'Big Kid'].

Game two's was Fed-Exed to me at my hotel ["Concierge? Is this a secure line? Yes, I'm expecting something very important to arrive in the morning. There might be a buck in it for you if all goes according to plan..."].

Wrigleyville was unusually kinetic the night of the opening game with the Marlins. The weather was autumnal and the clear night sky featured a big moon. The ivy vines on the outfield walls were actually turning red, yellow and orange; shades I'd never seen there that made the place even more fetching. She was rising to the occasion of this extra season and the attention that came with it at a normally dormant time of the year.

When I took my seat in Section 235; Row 12, I discovered that I'd randomly landed next to a guy who'd once lived in Des Moines and patronized my pub. We weren't personally acquainted, but a lively dialogue sprang up between us fueled by our shared sense of the big event. Our conversation was enthused but not profane or otherwise offensive, so we were both taken aback when an annoyed woman in front of us turned around to ask, "Don't you two ever stop talking? Is there anything about baseball you *DON'T* know?"

What the hell was she doing there?

The game was an action packed roller coaster. The Cubs broke in front 4-0 in the 1st inning only to fall behind when the Marlins scored five times in the 3rd. The Cubs retook the lead and again relinquished it by giving up two runs in the top of the 9th. But Sosa hit a dramatic, game-tying home run with two outs in the bottom of the ninth when he was all that stood between his team and defeat. The noise was too much for the ears so it burst through them and ran like a fuel through my entire body. I could feel it and it felt good; like tapping into a powerful force.

Florida finally won the game 9-8 in 11 innings. Between them the teams sprayed a constellation of seven homers into the night. I was drained and crestfallen and supposed that the Cubs must be too. But the encore they staged the next night suggested not.

The Cubs scored early and often - two in the 1st, three in the 2nd, then three more in the 3rd. Mark Prior was toying with the Marlins and the lead ballooned to 11-0 by the 5th inning. Home runs were flying into the heavens again, all but exploding into pyrotechnic blossoms at their apogees. Another half dozen were launched, four of them by the Cubs. Sosa tagged one in the 2nd inning that ricocheted off the camera shed deep in the center field bleachers like a sandlot blast crashing through a biddy's window two yards away.

There was no stopping the Cubs this night and they coasted to a muscle-flexing 12-3 victory. I was feeling both joyous and selfish when the energized crowd spilled into the neighborhood to celebrate. Shouldn't I have brought the kids along to share in this? My guilty conscience was overcome two ways: For one thing, the cost of including them would have been prohibitive. I'd paid my dues; they could wait. But the greater justification was the scene outside the ballpark after just one of the four wins it would take just to qualify for the World Series.

Curbside trash barrels were aflame. People were dancing atop city buses. Squeezing onto the "L" was like squeezing into the bar scene from *Star Wars*. Strange creatures abounded. Even sober folks like me were drunk on the Cubs. Frankly, I was glad not to be worried about the safety of young children.

The next morning I arose early and wound my way through the teeming traffic of an exultant city that brimmed with anticipation.

I drove merrily home, the back seat laden with exotica; NLCS t-shirts and beaded necklaces, placards and leaflets distributed by street people outside the ballpark, commemorative cups and game programs, etc. I had been to the mountaintop and glimpsed the Promised Land beyond. Deliverance was at hand and the safest place to watch it was at home, complete with instant replays.

Somewhere along this six month road I'd apparently told the kids that if the Cubs made it to the World Series I'd color my silver hair blue, strip naked and skip down the middle of Ingersoll Ave., the main traffic artery just a block south of our home. This prospect delighted them and now loomed in their minds as the chief perk should the Cubs finish off the Marlins and capture the National League flag. For me it was a suddenly very real tax I stood to pay as soon as the formality of three more wins was accomplished. If I had to be jailed as ransom for the realization of a dream, so be it. Besides, my own excitement was tempered by recollection of the 1984 playoff collapse at the hands of the San Diego Padres. The Cubs had won the first two games at home in convincing fashion when there was only one, best-of-five playoff round between the regular season and the Series. Then they crash-landed in California. Until then, no team had won the first two games and lost the next three. The Cubs did.

So I'd believe they were in the Series when I saw it.

When they won games three and four in Florida I could feel my hair starting to tint and my clothes falling away like the loser at a strip poker table. I started to stretch and loosen up and told the kids that the timing of my victory lap was up to me, reasoning that a middle-of-the-night dash would satisfy the letter if not the spirit of the dare I'd thrown down to the fates.

When the Cubs lost game five it only ensured that they would return to Chicago for the coronation with Mark Prior and Kerry Wood slotted to pitch the next game[s].

I foolishly puckered up when Death smooched Cubland with a curse disguised as reassurance: the Cubs hadn't lost consecutive games all year that were pitched by Prior and Wood.

Game six of the 2003 NLCS was the cruelest endured by Cub fans since the fifth and final game of that historically tragic series with the Padres in '84.

Prior held the Marlins at bay while his teammates built a 3-0 lead. In the top of the eighth he retired the leadoff man routinely, the 22nd out of the game. Only five more and the Cubs would be in the World Series for the first time since 1945.

Then a foul ball popped down the 3rd baseline headed in the general direction of an unsuspecting schmuck who probably had been reflecting throughout the game on what a great seat he had, especially for such a big game! And now here came a foul ball; what a great souvenir and story that would make!

He stood and extended his mitted hand in greeting like an innocent opening the door at the unrecognizable knock of the bogeyman.

The ball never got to the poor guy's glove.

Nor did it settle in Moises Alou's. Alou had charged over from his post in left field hoping to make putout #23. Instead he scowled at the fan who wore the same cap on his head that Alou did on his.

Oh well. Where were we?

Seldom have floodwaters risen so quickly.

Within the next several minutes the Marlins plated eight runs and struck the stage of a carnival scene. Wrigley Field fell tomb-like.

The guy who tried to catch the foul ball left early and empty-handed, not to mention under guard for the sake of his personal safety.

Meanwhile back at our house I'd crept ever nearer the TV screen as the nightmarish inning unfolded. I was nose-to-nose with the horror show by the time it broke for a commercial.

The rest of it is a blur. The next thing I remember is taking a phone call out on the front porch from my Uncle Jim who'd been retired for many years in Florida. He didn't call to gloat. He called in sympathy, but I was in shock and impervious to his stabs at consolation.

There was still tomorrow but I awaited it now as a condemned man awaits the serving of his last meal.

Game seven was an act of desperation for the Cubs who scurried about on the field like trapped prey.

The Marlins took an early lead. The Cubs came back to tie it up when Wood crushed a home run in the bottom of the 2nd, bringing the crowd to its feet in an ovation that was more beseeching than confident. But Wood's job was to pitch, not hit, and he wasn't up to it. He was gone by the sixth inning and so were the Cubs' chances. The team had collapsed like a runner cramping up just short of a marathon's finish line. The whole glorious season went as abruptly flat as a cake taken too soon from the oven.

The innocent dupe who'd risen to meet the foul ball late in game six was held more accountable in many quarters than the team itself. He was linked in the voodoo of the Cubs' hapless history to the curse of the billy goat which is too preposterous and trite to be recounted again here. No, baseball is a game that lends itself to precise, numeric analysis and an autopsy of that sort makes coldly clear what accounted for the breathtaking demise of the 2003 team just as it seemed poised to liberate the organization's faithful legions from the dungeon of futility.

I come from the town where the first night game under permanent lights in the history of professional baseball was played on May 2, 1930. It is no accident that Des Moines has not become as storied for demonstrating nocturnal baseball as has Kitty Hawk for pushing man from the nest of planet earth. That game between the Des Moines Demons and the Wichita Aviators may have seemed a good idea at the time, but it has led directly, if methodically, to such plagues as roofed ballparks, fake grass and World Series games that end in the middle of the night.

Wrigley Field was the last bastion of matinee ballgames. But it finally fell into the abyss when lights were erected there and a night game was scheduled for the first time on 8/8/88. There was the last warning of a rainout that evening, but it went unheeded.

Do you not see it? When the Cubs came close enough to taste the champagne of the 2003 National League pennant, what happened? *EIGHT* runs in the *EIGHTH* inning. Forget the foul pop; the key play in that inning was a botched double play ball that would have nipped it in the bud. Who made the critical error? The Cubs' shortstop Alex Gonzales; #8. The series with the Marlins began on October 7 and ended on October 15, a period of *EIGHT* days.

Intervention of the fates was not required in either 1989 or 1998 when lesser editions of the Cubs advanced beyond the regular season. The Giants and Braves were simply better teams in those cases. But this time a point was made when the fledgling franchise from the *SUNSHINE* state was smiled upon.

At home there ensued a period of spiritual convalescence commensurate with the depth of the wound.

My sympathetic, sarcastic wife clipped from the local paper a cartoon that depicted a horrified Cub fan on his knees in front of a television, eyes big as saucers, hands pulling out hair. She displayed it on the refrigerator; the perfect caricature/portrait of her sad- sack husband.

The kids, Max and Ben especially, regarded me unsurely for a while. I was given both physical and emotional space. They knew I'd been aggrieved somehow, but could not fully appreciate my sense that I had now missed out on the two most golden chances in my lifetime to see the Cubs on the World Series stage. The good news appeared to be that the core of the team was still young and on the come; the window of opportunity and potential remained open. I knew better. It had been nearly two decades between the Padre and Marlin tragedies. The boys were young but I couldn't take for granted that I had two more decades in me.

We were also at cross purposes in the sense that my consolation in this scenario was their major disappointment: there would be no blue-haired streaker skipping down the avenue.

As that autumn chilled toward winter I was confronted with a paternal dilemma. I wanted on some level to impart to my children a hopefulness about the future, not saddle them with their old man's fatalism. But it wasn't in me just then. I'd had more baseball that year than ever before. And for at least the long, bitter winter that lay ahead, it was more than enough.

Come Blow Your Horn

There was a soundtrack developing behind Max's life as he neared teenhood.

During that last little league season we saw notices in the newspaper of auditions for the Heartland Youth Choir, a new organization under the direction of a maestro he knew from his earlier days in youth choir.

Max declared his desire to try out and he went straight to his audition from a ballgame; a choirboy in cleats. His voice was changing and so, squeaky. Still, he was placed in the highest of the organization's five tiers, a chamber choir comprised almost exclusively of high schoolers. Max was the youngest; sort of a mascot.

He was also a trumpeter of some promise when he traveled with Chris to Minneapolis to see Doc Severinsen perform with the Minnesota Orchestra on November 15, 2003. They went at the invitation of my cousin's wife who was a cellist in the host orchestra; someone we'd met and connected with at the family reunion a few years prior.

We were a month removed from the Cub tragedy. I was back from catatonia and taking solid foods; even walking around a bit and leaving the house occasionally. The doctors must have given Chris the go-ahead to leave me overnight. I was placed in the care of Ben and Emma while my wife and our first-born took a walk on the finer side.

After the concerto Mina arranged for Max to go backstage where he got to meet Severinsen and have a ticket stub autographed. He came home suitably impressed.

Our son was coming to a turning point in his life and from my passenger seat I could see which direction the arrow was pointing. We were headed down a road I'd not traveled and I was both curious to see where it would lead and a little apprehensive since I couldn't provide direction.

Over the course of my relatively brief parenting career I'd come to believe that God passed out the gifts and left it to us to open and appreciate them. He cast the stars and made out the lineups; we bought and sold the tickets. I'd made Max a baseball fan in my own image and in return, he was gonna make me a patron of the arts.

Life is drawn by countless fine lines. One of them runs between a father sharing his beliefs and interests and imposing them.

I couldn't have concealed my Cub problem from the kids even if I'd thought to try. The Cubs were just another bad habit in some ways and had been filed under my life's unfinished business by the time I had children.

I absorbed them from my father without getting the idea that it was important to him that I be a ballplayer myself. Playing the game had more to do with my big brother and neighborhood pals. I wasn't bad. I played hard and always got my uniform dirty. I made the Raccoon Valley All-Stars [and struck out with the bases loaded to end our one-and-done run in the county tournament] and my dad was at every game I ever played in. But his involvement beyond that was limited to shagging foul balls and returning them to the umpire. He never coached. We played catch sometimes but I don't recall any real instruction he imparted as to the mechanics of hitting, catching and throwing.

I noticed that he admired hustle and loathed showboating, two principles that collided when Pete Rose came along. Right away I think dad smelled a skunk. He should have applauded the way "Charlie Hustle" sprinted to 1st base when he'd drawn a walk, but instead it was perceived as hot-dogging. When Rose would dive into a gratuitous belly flop slide without a play being made on him my dad would shake his head in disdain, extending an arm toward the TV and wagging a finger as though fending off something objectionable; as if to say, "mark my words...".

I learned a lot of what I still know and believe about baseball from my dad without him ever coaching me or suggesting in any overt, explicit way that it was really, truly important in the grander scheme.

Listening to a ballgame with him was like sharing a meal. We monitored the [mis]fortunes of our favorite team from afar by crackled radio broadcasts. The only time we sat together at Wrigley Field was late in his life and after I'd grown to [physical] adulthood, mostly because we couldn't afford to when I was a kid.

When Max and Ben reached the qualifying age for Little League I was unprepared. Subconsciously I subscribed to my dad's model, but, as noted earlier, times had really changed since I was a boy. Involvement at the forefront of a burgeoning array of organized activities for kids, even very young and small ones, was the new standard for conscientious parents; at least that was my perception.

I've already admitted that on some level I harbored the fantasy that my foals would be champions; I may even have taken somewhat for granted that they would exhibit some athletic facility - besides my modest exploits as a youngster, their mother played some ball in high school too - but it was hardly a priority. Early on the purity of my sheer fascination with each of them overrode any tendency to try and contrive their lives for them. I was more curious about who they were than determined to tell them who they'd be.

I took them to ballgames near and far because I could; I suspect my dad would have done the same given the means.

Max enjoyed watching ballgames with me; Ben liked to be outside playing them. While Max and I were inside arguing about some player or an umpire's call, Ben might be out in the front yard playing and announcing an imaginary game, spreading himself thin enough to represent both teams. Three oak trees stood in the approximate alignment of three bases and our house was even covered with vines!

But even as Max's musical talents began to emerge so did a certain physical clumsiness. He had flat feet and was either ambidextrous or dexterously ambiguous since neither arm readily emerged as the dominant one for throwing; both were scatterguns. Eventually he would write as a southpaw and pitch as a right-hander.

It was actually sort of endearing except that it clearly troubled him. I worried that I'd inflicted sports, baseball particularly, upon him, and that he fretted about not pleasing his father athletically. But I also feared talking frankly with him because I didn't want to be misconstrued as saying that he was wasting his time trying to be a ballplayer. I just wanted him to know that my fantasy was for the Cubs to play in the World Series; not for him to lead them there.

He was on the cusp of middle school where sports were cool and guys didn't sing. His trump card wasn't even in the deck.

Meanwhile Ben was just good enough to get us caught up in the maelstrom of AAU. He was part of a team that included his cousin and was coached by his uncle. Whatever angst this may have caused his older brother, Max kept to himself. The angst it caused his father sometimes slipped out at the wrong time in the wrong place like the verbal vomit of Turet's Syndrome, but for the most part I swallowed it and lay awake at night like someone in bed, if not necessarily sleeping with, the enemy.

On the one hand I had to admit that if, when I'd been nine, some grownups put together a team with names on the back of uniforms and matching gear bags and out-of-town tournament trips and trophies and medals and car windows soaped with uniform numbers and parents arguing with umpires and coaches, etc., I'd probably have been gung-ho. But then, I would still have been nine and what would I have known?

One of the problems with modern times is that there are so many, some of them aren't recognizable. What with terrorism and global climate change and spiraling health care costs and Lindsay Lohan, what chance is there that anyone will blow the whistle on little leaguers towing their $300 bats and gloves about in wheeled luggage like tycoons racing to make flight connections at a busy airport?

The only brand new bat I ever had was a 29" Al Kaline model Louisville Slugger that I selected in the basement of Hopkin's Sporting Goods before my last year at Raccoon Valley. It was made of wood, not the titanium or plutonium or whatever that's used these days to tide kids over until they're old enough for steroids.

We used to hang around the dugout at the neighborhood high school games hoping to get the cracked bats for salvage. We'd take 'em home, put a nail in the fracture, tape it over and use 'em on the sandlot. Best one I ever restored was busted by Gary

Mitzkoff, a Roosevelt High School slugger built along the lines of Hack Wilson [short but barrel-chested]. Wilson was a hard-hitting, hard-living Cub in the 1930's who still holds the major league record for RBI's in a single season [191].

The waters of parenthood were rising faster now. I took what fatherly refuge I could in Emma; blissfully simple and sweet and seven. My relationship with her still ran pretty well on a steady diet of mutual love and adoration. Taking my one and only daughter to the Valentine's Day Sweetheart Dance at the Val Air Ballroom and holding her aloft for a twirl around the dance floor was a breeze compared to what to do about the boys and baseball. With her brothers the plot had thickened to the point that more and more guidance was called for and I wasn't sure where to find it.

Time Out

One of the perks of parenting is that you get to live with people who change. And they change you. At least they should. I am still quite selfish but maybe less so than when this all began.

Teaching and learning go on at a dizzying pace and I think I've done more of the latter than the former. You can't teach what you don't know. I couldn't teach our children how to finesse a deal or fix the sink because I've never done either. I found it easier to dispense advice than to be a good example.

Still, our works in progress are just that; in progress. They are the living, breathing, walking, talking answers to the trite question: If you had it to do over again...

You think you have a shot at some redo, but they go mostly their own way like water seeking its own level.

Max always liked to debate. Ben was always looking for predictions. Emma would ask who to cheer for.

When we took them to the zoo Ben was drawn to sharks and polar bears. Max went for the primates and empathized. Emma fell for the big cats and elephants.

The inherent differences between them never fail to fascinate.

Their entertainments of us are sometimes trained and practiced; sometimes spontaneous and unwitting.

Once when Emma was acting out some sort of fairy princess fantasy in full improvised regalia [e.g., bath towel cape, feather duster wand, etc.] she inadvertently farted, paused and then further broke character to suggest to her audience: "how 'bout we just pretend that didn't happen?"

Another time in church the bored Ben resorted to a children's pamphlet of time-passers. Before beginning a rudimentary dot-to-dot exercise he appraised it for a moment and asserted, "50 bucks says this is Jesus." The prophet Benjamin! He and I also had a standing contest to see who could open the Hymnal and the Book of Common Prayer closest to the appointed pages. Page 323 of the

BCP where Rite One of The Holy Eucharist begins was a regular reference point and got to be one that we both homed in on pretty well. Every couple of weeks one of us would nail it on the nose.

Max has always declared his independence and Ben has always sought a wing man or two.

You start with a wide-angle panoramic view of the whole thing that narrows at the pace of a sunset in a world where a day lasts years until you are eclipsed and they become invisible; not out of earshot and not totally out of reach, but invisible except for what you think and remember of them.

Mere pictures lack the full dimension of memory and feeling; most of them are cheap imitations, parental taxidermy that runs a poor second to the menagerie that lives and runs in the heart and mind forever. Most don't do as much justice to the past as outgrown Batman and Power Ranger undies rediscovered in basement boxes.

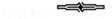

Getting Stung

Three days shy of my 50th birthday in 2004 Chris took me to see Sting at the Des Moines Civic Center. I'd seen him once previously somewhere in Des Moines in his role as chief of The Police at a much murkier stage of my life. Since then I'd cleaned up my own act considerably. Even so, had I taken a show on the

road billing myself as a verb/noun, the stage name would probably have been Belch, Fart or Yell. My utter non-musicality would
have killed any box office potential, though. It was probably best
that I'd become essentially a homebody by that point.

Two songs stung me that evening.

One was *Send Your Love*. It was elaborately staged. It pulsed and
throbbed and climbed to a crescendo of sound and light that was
encompassing. I chose to interpret the lyrics from a paternal perspective, reflecting on our children as love boomerangs being flung
further ahead in time than I'd be able to go but which would always, in a sense, come back to me. The part about there being "no
religion but sex and music" struck as a rather flamboyant and ris-
que world view, but given what concert tickets go for nowadays I
figure it's not only okay to take what you like and leave the rest; it
makes damn good sense! No different than cheering when Sosa hit
one out of the park and jeering when he missed the cutoff man.

The other tune that stayed with me in the aftermath of the show
was *Dead Man's Rope*. It was the sensory and spiritual flipside of
Send Your Love.

Here I was at 50 years old, 15 years married and 10 years sober;
feeling like I had landed on my feet after a freefall, but still a little
unsteady on them. The song talked about walking in a "circle of
addiction" and "walking away from Jesus' love." It struck the
same reflective mood that marked my life at that juncture and
gave me some pause.

Later that year our eldest child would become a teenager.

Somehow I'd been delivered from that phase of my own growth and development, but at what cost?

I wanted to be faithful but was more inclined to be fearful. Why? There was by then quite a body of evidence built up over my life's course to suggest that I'd never been left truly alone to my own devices [hallelujah!]. What consequences I'd suffered of bad choices and decisions were, on balance, commensurate to having minimum sentences imposed.

Never certain as to the mind and will of God, I was nevertheless at a point where I counted myself blessed and thought I knew who to thank. But there persisted some nagging notion that there might yet be the reaping that I truly deserved; that I would suffer as a father what I'd inflicted as a son.

There was nothing extant in my life that even hinted at that sort of arrangement. In fact, if somebody invoked the platitude that, "life isn't fair," in a spirit of complaint, my nods of agreement were in a spirit of gratitude and relief.

Still, past results are no guarantee of future success.

A Second Opinion

Not even a month later I was back at the Civic Center again, this time with Max. Doc Severinsen was in town touring with his big band as opposed to sitting in with a symphony orchestra as he'd done when Max and Chris saw him perform in Minneapolis.

Max's second exposure to the famed bugler in a period of four months came at my behest. It was a Tuesday night; a school night, and the place was probably a little past half of its 2,700 seat capacity.

I was by no means a fan of trumpeters in general or of Severinsen in particular. Chris Botti had opened for Sting, and frankly was more impressive that night than Doc was on this one. You see the up and comers and feel like you're getting in on the ground floor; you see the aging legends in a spirit of paying your respects. Actually, my favorite horn blower was Max and he did much of his tooting at school and in private lessons where I couldn't attend.

He was happy to accept my invitation but did not angle for it. It came his way unbidden, borne of my rising consciousness of his talents and interests and a desire to signal him that I was in full support. Sure son, I'm pretty much a hot dog and peanuts guy at events where booze and boos go hand in hand. But that doesn't mean I'm any more beyond refinement than crude oil.

Unable to teach Max anything about the fine arts I was determined that he know I was willing to learn from him.

There can be an arrangement between parents and offspring, particularly evident in cases of fathers and sons, whereby the elder sets the youngster's agenda. It's not a new dynamic; for practically ever the old man has wanted the kid to follow in his footsteps or take over the family business or be the first to go to college or work outside the mines.

The contemporary wrinkle on this age-old theme that I've noticed since becoming a father myself is that there's a greater than ever before emphasis on sports.

Once upon a time the old folks at home permitted the kids to amuse themselves with games on the sandlot and out in the driveway, but they were seen as childish things to be put away as adulthood drew near. Children of hard-working immigrants had to beg for permission when scouts came around waving contracts to play professional baseball. And of course, pre-Title IX, there was hardly such a thing as a female athlete outside of Babe Didrikson.

Isn't it interesting that now, even as the sporting public becomes ever more jaded and cynical; even as the sports page and the police blotter overlap as never before; even as the line between amateurism and professionalism blurs; even as athletes at all levels become more and more transient in their affiliations, moms and pops line up to sacrifice their kids' childhoods at the altar of organized sports as soon as they're able?

The immigrants of past generations steered their kids away from sports because there was no money in them. Now we flock to them because there's so much of it.

It's a strong current to swim against.

You don't want yours to be the only children on the block with free time on their hands after school. You don't want them to be without a personal trainer. What's the fun of playing exclusively with and against kids you see at school every day once you've reached the ripe old age of 10? What about athletic wanderlust, the call of the sporting wild? The hell with dinner-at-six monotony; what say the family hits the open road this weekend for the U9 regionals in Minneapolis - it's only a three-hour drive!?

There's a trendy axiom that peppers post-game interviews nowadays. Athletes are often heard to talk about letting the game come to them. If only we parents could.

Behind the Scenes

The long, dark offseason that was the winter of 2003-04 finally gave way to a spring that was more eagerly awaited than most at our house. The open wound of the Cubs' painful near miss last autumn had closed. There was emotional scar tissue, but like players rehabbing from serious physical injuries, us fans had worked hard to delude ourselves into thinking that in 2004 the team would kick down the door it had knocked on so hard in 2003.

At home, Ben had reached double digits in February and was eligible to try out for the majors at Raccoon Valley. He was drafted by the Cubs; an omen if ever I saw one. On a chilly Opening Day, the first Saturday in April, he lined a base hit to center in his first at-bat of the season. The pitcher he faced was a hard thrower and much bigger than Ben. I was impressed. Here we went again.

I planned yet another expedition to Chicago that would coincide roughly with the end of the school year; Chris' first as a teacher.

She'd gone back to school and finished a degree through a program of night classes. She was hired as a 1st grade teacher in the Des Moines public schools upon her graduation in the spring of 2003.

I was impressed by her too. The maternal tenderness she displayed with her own children extended reflexively to others. She was a natural and had found her niche easing kids into the routine of days spent away from home. She made a scary place feel safe and fun, all the while teaching them to read! Right away I envied her the importance and value of her job. In some ways it was like our family had expanded to include a couple dozen additional children. I got to know many of them just listening to Chris talk about them at home. She stretched herself like an accordion being played for the benefit of a bigger audience.

Her class that first year was the same age as our daughter. Though they were at different schools, it was as if Chris and Emma went through 1st grade together.

Luckily we did not have to house and feed Chris' students, nor did they accompany us on our trip over the Memorial Day weekend. It was all we could manage to subsidize and otherwise account for the three we bore full responsibility for.

STUBS

The Cubs were actually on the road when we arrived in Chicago but that made their playground available for behind-the-scenes tours. The boys and I signed on for the 3:00 group on Saturday, May 29th.

We'd been to many games at Wrigley Field but this visit was like prowling your attic or your parents' dresser drawers when they're not home.

We dot-to-dotted through the press box, the bleachers, the dugouts and the visiting team clubhouse. A point was made of stopping in the security force command center under the stands. There it was made clear that there was enough electronic surveillance going on at this place to catch you if you tried to stick a wad of gum under your seat in the midst of a capacity crowd. So don't even think about trying to undress Mona Lisa by plucking a leaf of ivy from the outfield walls.

We scratched our names in the infield dirt. We peed in the cramped urinal that's in the tunnel between the Cub dugout and their clubhouse. I pointed out to Max and Ben that they were relieving themselves in the very spot where Banks, Santo, Williams, Sandberg, Wood and Sosa had done the same thing. They lingered instead of impatiently zipping the last drops into their shorts.

The tour culminated when we reached the team's inner sanctum where the players dressed and undressed before and after games; their respite from the alternately adoring and unruly fans and the always probing press corps.

The clubhouse manager offered some insights into life as a big leaguer. He explained how little the ballplayers do for themselves and how much is done for them in exchange for their generous tips; everything from parking their cars to picking up their dry cleaning. He told us how Greg Maddux always came in early on the days he was to pitch for a big breakfast of pancakes. He revealed that Sammy Sosa always sent one of the clubhouse attendants across the street after batting practice on game days to fetch him a pair of Big Macs.

Afterwards we rejoined the girls for a dinner of stuffed pizza at a touristy joint on Rush Street that's so popular part of the routine there is the hour-long wait on the sidewalk outside. You order when you get there because the pies are so deep they take almost as long to bake as you have to wait for a table. But we always decide they have been worth our waiting when we remove a pennant of pepperoni from the whole and a tether of mozzarella stretches as long as your arm will allow, like a string on a bass fiddle that must be plucked in two. It is almost too gummy to be as good as we all swear it is. Once consumed the cheesy anvil sits in the gut for a time before continuing on its way through one's system like a case making its way through the courts.

Really the best ingredient of the whole thing is the sharing of it. Chicago pizza is one of the few foods the five of us agree upon.

We passed the next day expensively on The Magnificent Mile. Max hit the shop in Watertower Place to expand his collection of bobbleheads, Emma made the obligatory stop at The American Girl Place and Ben lusted indiscriminately after all sorts of merchandise up and down the avenue. For Chris and Emma the trip's primary purpose was served. The majority of us were biding time until the Cubs returned from Pittsburgh to host the Houston Astros in a holiday ballgame.

Well, at least Ben and I were. Max may have been more preoccupied with a coming trip to New York. His choir was going to sing at Carnegie Hall on June 15 and Chris was on board as a chaperone.

The choirboy son of a roguish baseball fan was about to take the field at the Yankee Stadium of music!

Us guys were up early on Memorial Day to beat the rush to the "L" and the ballpark. Ben seemed always to love the "just the three of us" aspects of our junkets to Chicago, but he was made uneasy by big crowds. Sometimes the middle of a standing room only throng on a train car seemed like a place where anything might happen, and even when nothing exceptional did, the shoulder to shoulder ambience left a livestockish taste in the mouth and made it hard for any random three heads in the herd to feel somehow special.

So this morning we strayed early and beat the rush, browsing the souvenir shops that front Addison between Clark and Sheffield and the temporary, portable stands that open and close like tulips on game days during the season.

Our visits to Wrigleyville were frequent enough that we had to become more discriminating souvenir shoppers, both because of costs and the fact that we had built up quite a stockpile of flotsam over the last few years. T-shirts, for instance, were quickly outgrown. Stuff with players' names on it was speculative given their transience and physical fragility. Better to traffic in merchandise that featured the ballpark; the rock on which the Cub brand was built.

We learned that hatpins were good values @ $5 apiece or 3/$12. Plus, they were collectibles and easy to carry on one's person throughout a long day at the fair.

Also compact and affordable were the vials of "Diamond Dust" mined from the infield dirt inside the ballpark. I choose not to believe that it was actually collected from the alleys behind the neighborhood bars and have given some thought to what might result if a portion is someday mixed with my ashen residue and sprinkled between second and third on a sandlot. Perhaps a short-stop would grow there.

Having made the rounds we still had money in our pockets and time on our hands. The gates to the ballpark wouldn't open yet for more than an hour so we decided to eat and rest at the McDonalds on Clark. As we jaywalked our way around and through traffic I noticed a fellow pedestrian who looked familiar and was clearly in a hurry. He wore a light blue oxford shirt, khakis, black walking shoes and a two-toned Cub cap; the uniform of a stadium employee.

It was the guy from the clubhouse on the tour! He too was headed for McDonald's.

"Hey! You going to get Sammy's Big Macs?" I hollered.

He grinned at us and we grinned at each other. Now knowing a secret, we got back in line with the rest of the herd.

The Cubs won that day. The winning pitcher was Greg Maddux, no doubt fortified by a hearty pancake breakfast. Sosa didn't play. He was on the disabled list, still recouping from back spasms induced by some Richter scale sneezes that had shaken him during a recent road trip to San Diego.

We took as an encouraging sign that he was back on his Big Macs.

Lone Ranging

I took Chris and Max to the airport to begin their great adventure to Gotham. Then I headed east by car, alone. They flew over and past me later that same morning en route to New York while I was somewhere on the path I'd worn between Des Moines and Chicago along Interstate 80.

My good fortune as a publican had afforded me the chance to become something of a baseball vagabond during these years that coincided with uncharacteristically good fortune for the Cubs. The team had become generally good enough to make its fans angry when it inevitably fell short. This reaction was instead of the wry smile and shrug of shoulders that used to accompany whole seasons of mediocrity. The club still hadn't been to the World Series since 1945, but expanded tiers of post-season playoffs had allowed the Cubs to extend the seasons of 1984, 1989, 1998 and 2003 beyond the regular limits and tease their fans cruelly before falling; still short of the ultimate prize but closer to it than had long been accepted as normal.

Raised on the cheap and harmless routine of listening to games from afar via radio, I was now getting into almost the habit of making a 700 mile round trip to attend games and incurring all of the related expenses.

What started innocently as the equivalent of penny-ante poker on the kitchen table had inflamed to the point of big-stakes junkets to the casino. I was all in.

This trip was enabled by some level of manipulation on my part. Playing on the good nature of my mother-in-law and her adoration of her grandchildren, I arranged for Ben and Emma to spend a couple of days at Grandma's house while I dashed to Chicago. The Cardinals were due in town. I promised to make it up to the stuck-at-home kids later in the summer and off I went!

I got to the ballpark on Wednesday, June 9 just in time to settle into a choice Club Box seat two rows behind the Cardinals' dugout. I expected to see Mark Prior toy with our archrivals in only his 2nd start back from rehabilitation of an injury to his Achilles tendon sustained during spring training.

Prior had pitched three times in the Cubs' minor league system on his way back from the injury. In fact, he'd pitched a fine game in Des Moines while we'd been in Chicago over the Memorial Day weekend, striking out 10 batters in front of a packed house. That game signaled that he was ready again for the big leagues and his one start at that level prior to this outing against St. Louis had been splendid. He'd tossed six scoreless innings at the Pittsburgh Pirates, walking no one and fanning eight on June 4.

So I was both disappointed and surprised when the Redbirds roughed him up to the tune of five runs in less than four full innings. Prior even walked five batters; extremely unusual for him.

Just about the best seats I ever had turned out to be for a stinker of a game. The Cubs got trounced, 12-4.

The next day my seat was worse, a Terrace Reserved in Section 204 down the leftfield line, but the view was still better. The Cubs responded in kind to their thumping of the previous day and won the game, 12-3. In an almost slapstick bottom of the 4th inning the Cubs scored 10 runs on 11 hits; nine of them in succession at one point! I remember laughing out loud to no one in particular since I was there by myself.

That night I celebrated by taking myself to the Royal George Theatre to see a staging of *Bleacher Bums,* a comedy conceived by Chicagoan Joe Mantegna about Wrigley Field regulars and the relationships that develop over the course of a season between a team and its fans and between the fans themselves. The recognizable star of the show was the station manager from *WKRP in Cincinnati;* the guy with the hair.

I thought it was a symbolic melding of my lifelong interest in the Cubs and my developing interest in the performing arts.

While I was at the Royal George in Chicago, Chris and Max were somewhere on Broadway taking in *The Lion King*, a story about cubs of a different sort.

I got back home ahead of the New York expedition, in plenty of time to retrieve Ben and Emma before picking up the rest of our temporarily far-flung family at Des Moines International.

When I saw the boy and his mother walking toward us in the terminal I could not tell at first that he was unalterably different from who he'd been a week ago. He was physically recognizable and also familiar in most other ways. But gradually in the days and weeks to come the change wrought upon him by his journey to the center of another world began to show.

Driving through downtown Des Moines at night, usually either to or from an Iowa Cubs ballgame, Max suddenly took notice of the comparative desolation there and wondered aloud about it. He couldn't quite articulate it yet, but it was clear that he'd been smitten by the bright lights and footlights of the Big City.

I chuckled to think that this was the same kid who'd pedaled out the driveway not so long ago, bound for the home of a pal, only to abruptly return, sheepishly asking for directions on how to get to a place where he'd been many times, but never as the pilot.

How were we gonna keep him down on the farm now that he'd seen New York, New York?

Three Generations

After barely two weeks at home in Des Moines, we were back on the road again. This time the boys and I had invited their Grandpa Rick along for the ride to see the Cubs do battle with the Houston Astros.

We had tickets for all three games of the series. I'd bought them and was also doing the driving; Grandpa was on the hook for room and board [and, his grandsons took for granted, souvenirs more lavish than hatpins].

Max and Ben were old enough to have figured out that their maternal grandfather was more of a gadabout than their dad. Rick had a flamboyance about him that was made even less grandfatherly by the fact that he's less than a decade older than me [I'm 13 years older than his daughter, my wife]. He'd golfed at Doral and Super Bowled in Vegas. When the kids put together their Christmas lists each year they knew who to hit up for the big ticket items.

The four of us had never been to Wrigley together and Rick was excited at the invitation. We picked him up early on the morning of Tuesday, June 29 and arrived in Chicago that afternoon with plenty of time on our hands before the night game scheduled on that date.

After checking into our downtown lodgings we strolled to Harry Caray's nearby restaurant for lunch. Rick ordered a burger. Ben opted for his standard grilled cheese and fries. I think I had a club sandwich. Then came Max's turn. He seemed concerned as he perused the menu. Finally he looked up at his grandfather.

"Is it okay if I have the filet?" he asked.

Rick grinned at Max and then at me.

Max's taste for the finer cuts had actually been cultivated by his Grandpa Jerry. Some years after Rick and Joyce divorced they both remarried and Joyce and her husband Jerry vacationed with us at Minnesota lakes in the summertime. We'd fish and boat and swim and eat modest home-cooked meals all week like spaghetti and hot dogs on the grill. But on the last night of the week Jerry would splurge on some good steaks. Max acquired a taste for beef tenderloin. His lunch order in Chicago was equal parts where he'd been and where he planned to go.

"Sure, anything you want," said Grandpa Swashbuckle.

Max ate every last bite.

Our tickets for the game that night were upper deck box seats down the leftfield line; on the aisle in the 3rd row of Section 406.

At Wrigley Field you hike to the upper deck; there are no elevators or escalators. The walk up the concrete ramps that climb from street level to the steep seats is a real trudge. Finally it spills out on a panoramic view encompassing everything from the ballhawks on Waveland Avenue to the emerald diamond of the field to the broad-shouldered city skyline to the oasitic waters of Lake Michigan. You find yourself in a spot above the gulls but still within range of foul balls glancing off of bats far below. A would-be clout, like a litter runt going to a good home, is as prized here as are home runs in the bleachers.

It's a matter of record that the Cubs won that evening's game by a score of 7-5. I had to look that up. Nothing else stuck.

By the time we got off the train back downtown it was late and Wednesday's game was a matinee. Over the course of the long season it's not uncommon for baseball managers to rest a couple of the lineup regulars in day games following nighttime ones, especially once the dog days of mid-summer roll around. But there's no rest for the fans, certainly not for touristy ones like us. Our self-imposed curfew was as soon as we could get back to the hotel and bed down. The elders fell quickly asleep despite the din of the excited third generation. It had been a long day and night of cars and trains and crowds. One down, two to go.

Day two was blue-skied. The sun broke the horizon and just kept rising. It was a perfect day for the bleachers and that's just where we were, back again in the Family Section of the leftfield corner. On our way to Wrigley Grandpa saw to it that the boys were out-fitted for the occasion when we stopped at a souvenir shop on the corner of Addison & Sheffield. From there we made our way to Waveland for an obligatory session of ballhawking. Some catch was played in the street while we waited for balls to start raining from the sky, but none did.

We had better luck inside. An Astro shagging balls in the outfield during batting practice fetched one that had rolled to a stop on the crushed red rock of the warning track and tossed it up to Ben.

It had a big black "H" scrawled on it as though the visitors had brought their own balls with them from Houston.

Roger Clemens was pitching that day for the Astros. He turned in a solid seven innings of work but did not figure in the decision as his team won, 3-2, and evened the series at a game apiece.

The game was tied into the 9th inning when the Astros' recently acquired centerfielder, Carlos Beltran, homered for the deciding run. In the bottom of the 9th Houston closer Brad Lidge retired the Cubs in order and the ballpark emptied quietly except for a collective grumble of disappointment that sounded like the last of a tubful of water glugging down the drain.

Our foursome replenished on rib dinners downtown and took consolation in the prospect of Mark Prior pitching for our side the next day in the finale. The day's defeat was pushed further from our minds by dessert at the ESPN Zone. Max and Ben rode motorcycles, surfed, boxed, played hockey, shot free throws, tossed footballs and skied until their pass cards and chaperones were exhausted.

I slept as well that night as I am able to on the road while sharing a hide-a-bed with a kicking, covers-tugging youngster in the wake of a Cub loss sustained in the last inning. It was a good thing that I was not penciled into Thursday's lineup.

After a day in the bleachers we were lucky to sit the next day more or less directly beneath where we'd been for the night game that opened the three-game set. Our tickets directed us to the first three seats in the 7th row of section 208; very comfy with good sight lines.

Prior was workmanlike and by the time he took the mound for the top of the 8th the Cubs were in command to the tune of a 4-1 lead. The outcome seemed assured. To that point the only blemish on Prior's log was a solo homer by the redoubtable Beltran who'd now homered in each of the three games in Chicago less than a week after being traded to the Astros by the Kansas City Royals. Seldom does a traded player so quickly and emphatically ingratiate himself with new teammates.

Beltran was due up 4th in the 8th inning and by the time it was his turn he stepped to the plate representing the potential tying run.

Cub skipper Dusty Baker sensed that his pitcher was tiring and called southpaw reliever Kent Mercker in from the bullpen to quell the uprising.

The switch-hitting Beltran, whose other homers in the series had come while batting left-handed now hopped to the opposite batter's box to swing from the other side. Generally speaking, hitters at the major league level do better swinging from the side of the plate opposite the arm the pitcher throws with; something to do with the geometry of a pitch's approach and the point at which the batter's eye picks up the flight of the ball.

You could have heard a beer cup drop when Beltran blasted a three-run homer to tie the game. He circled the bases while Mercker pawed the dirt on the mound in a futile attempt to dig himself an escape tunnel.

The game prolonged into extra innings. The crowd was getting antsy. The four of us were facing the suddenly less appealing prospect of a long drive home right after the game.

Houston called on Lidge again to pitch the bottom of the 10th. He was one of the league's best relief pitchers and just the day before had put the Cubs to bed with no shenanigans in sealing his team's triumph.

While Lidge took the customary warmup pitches and the infielders and outfielders behind him tossed balls back and forth and people all around the park hustled to the bathrooms to give back the residues of their concessions, Sammy Sosa went through his own preparatory ritual near the Cub dugout. He was due to lead-off against Lidge.

Some at-bats and innings are chess-like battles between pitcher and batter; between manager and manager. Baseball in general is a methodical, strategic game that usually proceeds gradually to its resolution like a vehicle easing to a stop. But not always.

Sosa's only hit in 12 previous at-bats during the series was a harmless single. This time he leapt at the first pitch Lidge threw like a famished dog snatching at raw meat. From our vantage point the mind's eye instantly extrapolated that the ball was bound for Waveland Avenue. By the time the sound of the blast reverberated throughout the grounds every able body was already standing and Lidge was probably groping for the entrance to Mercker's tunnel.

Sheer elation surely courses through the hitter at such an instant.

The bat itself must feel it and there was enough of the stuff circulating at Wrigley Field in those next moments to emotionally electrocute 40,000 people. The voltage between and amongst the four of us peeled all of our eyes and mouths as open as they could be and electrified the many high-fives that passed between us. We smacked palms so hard the claps felt like jumper cables sparking at the touch. For just that moment three generations were blended into a composite boyhood thrill.

Later the question of whether or not cork and steroids somehow diluted that and the rest of the exploits of Sosa and his contemporaries was raised by the trickle of revelations and innuendos that leaked steadily into the sports pages.

All I'm certain of that's germane to this story is the joy that fueled our drive home from the big leagues that night was natural and pure.

Who's With Me?

I had one more batch of tickets left for that 2004 season. My almost compulsive Cub ticket hoarding had advanced to the point that I was grabbing them up when they went on sale in February and planning the trips to use them later.

The team had become bizarrely popular since my schoolboy days. When I was 12 the Cubs drew less than a million fans per season to their ballpark. Now they were playing to virtually capacity crowds on a daily basis and more than three million of us suckers were flocking to Clark & Addison every summer; some of us more than once - after all, I lived just down the road a few hundred miles.

When tickets went on sale I figured any I got my hands on would be sellable on E-bay if nothing else. Besides, buying baseball tickets in February was like spying robins in the yard, albeit more costly.

I had scored three apiece for games on Thursday and Friday August 26th and 27th. Again the opponent was the Astros, an emerging divisional rival, and again the seats were in the soft drinking Family Section of the bleachers.

The problem was finding somebody to go with me. Too close to the start of the school year for Chris. She was busy preparing her classroom. Max was at summer camp that week with school chums. Ben and Emma drew the assignment.

The three of us had never been on so elaborate an outing together. Emma was excited by the element of shared adventure but naïve as to the portion of the trip that would be spent either on the road or at the ballpark. Ben didn't see why Emma needed to come along, but if she behaved herself, well, alright.

His grudging tolerance of Emma's presence changed when we arrived at the ballpark on Thursday afternoon.

Players shagged batting practice balls scattered around the

outfield below us like children picking up their rooms. For them it was part of the day-to-day drudgery of the six-month season. For us, even after repeated visits, it was a chance to pick up a piece of personal history. Ben and I hailed them like drooling pooches begging table scraps, but they were deaf to our whines.

Emma was a different story. She didn't really care about the balls, but getting her hands on something her most immediate big brother desired sparked her interest. And the voice of a little girl stood out to the ballplayers like a siren amongst the deeper, impatient; even rude male pleas cascading down from the bleachers.

Thanks to Emma we hauled in practically a backpack full by the time batting practice ended. Naturally, Ben's gratitude expressed itself in arguments as to who should actually take custody of the day's catch. I was the third man in the ring, doing the best I could to keep the bout civilized. I enlisted the help of concessionaires as corner men to cool down the fighters. By the time the game began we united against a common enemy - the Astros.

The Cubs eased to an 8-3 win despite yet another homer from Carlos Beltran, the traded refugee from Kansas City who continued to lay waste to the Cubs and the rest of the National League. Sosa obliged the home fans with another roundtripper of his own.

It was a good day, one we topped off with a swim, some room service pizza and a movie back at the hotel.

All three of our kids have always taken to life on the road. Once we drove west for a summer stay with relatives in Colorado. We stopped for the night in North Platte, Nebraska, the approximate halfway point, and checked into a Holiday Inn Express hard by the interstate. When we unlocked the door to our room the crew raced to the curtains and yanked them wide open, unveiling a thoroughly bleak panorama that suggested the aftermath of a nuclear blast: a vacant lot devoid of vegetation; marked only by the occasional bag of fast food litter or uprooted scrub brush crossing it ushered by prairie winds that were as anxious to blow through Nebraska as most travelers.

"WHAT A VIEW!" they exclaimed in unison.

Not only that, "There's a bathroom in here!" Ben announced.

You can imagine the joy when we bunked at a property equipped with vending machines on every floor.

That night I ping-ponged between Ben and Emma in a king-sized bed, getting not nearly the rest I would need to keep pace with them for the next 36 or so hours. It was like martial arts lying down except that their kicks and thrusts were accompanied by grunts and snores rather than primal shrieks of, *"HI-YAA!"*

As Thursday became Friday I withdrew myself from the family sandwich, showered and slipped out to fetch a breakfast of doughnuts and chocolate milk for my companions and coffee and a newspaper for me while they slept on. If I couldn't be rested it was critical that they be.

Emma's delight at the breakfast in bed she awoke to was nullified during the morning briefing when she was reminded that the day's itinerary consisted primarily of another visit to the ballpark. And oh yeah, hurry up, let's get out there early!

We trained to Addison ahead of the rush of the game crowd, disembarked and walked out of the station headed down the block of sidewalk that runs parallel to the 1st baseline between Clark and Sheffield. It's the stretch where cabs pull up to drop off visiting ballplayers. Teams in town to take on the Cubs don't usually arrive at the ballpark together on a bus. Knowing this, serious memorabilia collectors and autograph hounds often gather there to ambush the objects of their collections.

On this particular morning, just as the traffic light blinked from don't walk to walk and we crossed Sheffield, a cab pulled over to the curb maybe 20 yards up ahead. Out stepped Astro star Craig Biggio.

Biggio was one of the opposing players I'd always admired.

He'd started out as a rookie catcher before later moving to 2nd base, an odd career arc that spoke to both his athleticism and his commitment to the team. Later he became a centerfielder and now, in the waning days of a long and illustrious run through the green fields of the big leagues, he was mostly positioned as a leftfielder, a spot that required less mobility and speed than 2B and CF and was less defensively critical than either of them or catcher.

Biggio's uniform usually got dirty during a game. His bat seemed especially wooden, covered as it always was with sticky pine tar and marked in its middle - the sweet spot - by a darker grain that I thought made it look stronger, though Biggio was never a slugger; more of a hustling doubles hitter with occasional home run power. His batting helmet was grimy, coated it seemed with infield dirt varnished on permanently with a coating of pine tar. He played by his wits and hard.

His overall style and presentation represented a living, breathing portrait of the kind of ballplayer I remembered myself having been as a youngster.

I assumed Ben would want his autograph.

The three of us grabbed hands and I tugged and towed the other two to the fringe of the cluster of early birds that formed around the players' entrance gate. Once he reached that threshold of sanctuary Biggio stopped and turned to oblige at least a portion of the small throng.

Ben was too small to thrust himself into the forefront so I bent over to grab him around the waist and raise him up. I was 50. Ben was 10. We were acting each other's ages. As soon as I hoisted him I knew I had trouble. Instead of a small voice inside whispering to me that I was too old for this, a sharp pain in my back yelled that at me. I held Ben aloft as long as I could, but it wasn't long; certainly not long enough to get the attention of Biggio before he turned on his heel and continued on his way to work.

I suffered through the game, and not just because the Cubs dropped a 15-7 slugfest in which the elegant Beltran not only racked up two more homers [giving him seven in the five games I'd seen him play that summer vs. the Cubs] but also stole two bases! He was playing like Willie Mays in his prime. Kerry Wood, who'd once fanned 20 Astros in a game, got cuffed around this day.

My aching back imposed a rather crooked posture on me but the pain was manageable as long as I was sitting down.

I noticed on the scoreboard before the game that the umpiring crew was not the same one that worked the game the day before. Ordinarily a crew is assigned a series at a time, but the second of this four-game set with Houston would be overseen by the four-some that included Eric Cooper from Des Moines. He was making the calls at first base. I hoped he called 'em as I saw 'em.

By then I'd mostly stopped angling for tickets through Eric. Once I watched a game at Wrigley sitting in a great seat in the Field Box section behind the plate, courtesy of him.

In the bottom of the 1st that day, he called a Cub base-stealer out at 2nd base on a close play. No problem; you win some, you lose some. But when the Cubs emerged from their dugout to take the field for the top of the 2nd inning, the thief must have shouted the magic word[s] at Eric all the way from the dugout steps to short right field. Eric threw him out of the game at a range of 50 or so yards - in the top of the 2nd!

I felt like I had a conflict of interest sitting there in a choice seat as the guest of the villain who'd just thrown our leadoff hitter out of the game practically before it began.

Eric was a professional working in a field that was an amusement, albeit a lifelong one, for me. I respected his achievement and was even jealous of his career highlights - he'd worked the plate in a couple of no-hitters and was on the crew for Cal Ripken's last game; later he'd work the last game at the original Yankee Stadium; the one that Ruth built - but he saw the game from a perspective now that struck me as jaundiced. I was already umpiring an internal contest between romanticism and cynicism with regard to my own attitudes about baseball and, I had to admit, I wanted the romantic side to win. But the cynics had fat, guaranteed contracts and labor disputes and steroids and corked bats and gambling managers on their side. I wanted to believe in something that I cherished from afar. Eric knew from being up close that it didn't exist.

I scrawled out a note to him to let him know that we were there and wish him and his mates a shift free from confrontation [the Cubs and Astros had already fought a bean ball war that still simmered] and had it delivered to the umps' locker room via the customer service window on the main concourse.

For us the game was a special day at the ballpark, the sound defeat of our favorite team notwithstanding. For the umps it was just another day at the office.

Our trio spent that night too in Chicago. While Ben and Emma slept my back stiffened. By the time we arose Saturday morning I was in the grip of a rigor mortis that crept up my spine leaving the rest of me intact enough to feel the pain. Luckily I was able to maneuver myself into the cockpit of the car for the drive home and grin and bear convincingly enough that the kids could devote themselves to arguments with one another about what movies to watch during the ride.

STUBS

The scene when we arrived home was that one from the westerns where the cowboy's pony trots up to the hitching post in front of the cabin with his wounded rider slumped over the saddle horn.

I made it up to bed but had no chance of getting out of there on Sunday morning. Whatever hope I had that this spasm would pass without medical attention was gone. The next day was the first day of school for Chris and the kids. It looked like the family bus driver would be out of commission.

I had to slink, snake-like, to the floor and crawl across it to the bathroom when that was where I needed to be. When I got there I was faced with the dilemma of how to get myself into position to reach the toilet. Dockings in outer space were more easily engineered than my droppings and drainings that weekend. The things we take for granted.

On Monday, after everyone left to launch the new school year, my mother-in-law arrived to transport me to the doctor. It took perhaps half an hour to get myself to her car. When we arrived at the doc's office I wobbled inside with the countenance of a gunshot victim. Sensing the urgency of my plight a receptionist ordered a full series of redundant forms - *STAT!* Then I was whisked over to have my height and weight checked; maybe one or both of them was the problem. Ah hah! My records indicated I was 6'1," but I was topping out this morning at about 5'6" - either I was an impostor or something else was crooked, like *MY ACHING BACK!* Closer examination by an actual doctor confirmed my suspicion; my back was killing me!

"You might have thought this tedious, uncaring processing here at the office was a pain in the neck," he intoned uncaringly, "but I'm afraid the real problem is muscle spasms in your back."

Just knowing officially what we were dealing with lifted a weight from my shoulders that in turn allowed my spine to begin straightening. Toss in a few days of muscle relaxers and I was back in game shape. No more infantry crawls to the spittoon.

I'd feared the injury was season-ending, but now nothing would keep me out of the post-season playoffs. Except the Cubs. Not long after I stood back up they collapsed in the final week of the regular season and missed the party.

The hell with baseball; the hell with the Cubs. They were a bad habit that was getting worse when you considered the lengths and expenses I was now going to just to indulge my masochistic preoccupation with them.

Every season was an expedition that broke down. I braced for another discontented winter.

This particular off-season brought larger issues to the forefront. At home Max was entering his last year of middle school and Ben his last at the elementary level. We were in transition. On the national scene an election loomed; my citizenship extended beyond the Cub nation, affording me the chance to hop off of their bandwagon and onto another steaming out of Massachusetts. Unfortunately, it wasn't the Red Sox'.

It was a good time for a taking of stock and so is this.

Intermission

I'd been a father long enough to see happening what I'd always known eventually would. Miraculous babies become cute toddlers become smart alec kids become awkward adolescents, etc. The inexorability of it all is at once fascinating and frustrating. You realize you've created monsters; not the kids themselves - their lives! At first wholly yours, children get slipperier until a lot of what you're left holding is responsibility and worry.

In between the succession of ticketed events that are recalled here as checkpoints along a retraced route, lots of things were happening to Max, Ben and Emma, and most of them were away from our view and beyond our seemingly shrinking powers. How the hell do any of us make it?

By 8th grade Max was coming to terms with the likelihood that his future was not as an athlete. It was clear that he possessed both talent and passion for music, but he kept his vocal skills and aspirations closeted at school. There he was content to play trumpet in the jazz band and tread the social waters, trying to stay afloat until high school where he reasoned there would be a general broadening of consciousness and opportunities that might work in his favor.

We tried to help boost him to at least a moderate level of popularity by allowing him to host a Halloween party that year. A list of guests was drawn up; a few basic ground rules were agreed upon; the house was cleaned and decorated and the spooky night arrived.

From the start there were uninvited crashers. Some of them were rather boldly confrontational with Chris at our front door while I was shuttling Ben and Emma out of the way over to grandma's as the shindig got underway. Others lurked in the shadows across the street, taunting and baiting throughout the evening. As closing time neared I saw a sihouette walk across the street and strike a pose of defecation in the approach to our driveway. I thought it was just a vulgar pantomime until I saw droppings fall from the hindquarters.

I raced outside and gave sprinted but brief pursuit. I was in adrenalized shock and disbelief when I returned home to clean up the party favor left by the human dog. Gee, why didn't Max invite him?

I'm not sure what would have been the wisest course of response. DNA testing of a fecal sample? Collaboration with school authorities on an investigation to identify the poopatrator? Immediate disbanding of the party? Nothing would have undone the sense of invasion I felt in the moment. Chris and I had to balance our retribution reflex against the potential for Max to sustain lasting repercussions in the hallways of middle school which can sometimes be more like sewer tunnels.

We gathered the invited guests and grilled them as to the identity of *The Crapper*. Even the kids seemed aghast at what had happened but no one knew for certain who was responsible. I calmed down and the party ran its course. If it had any lasting impact on

Max's social standing one way or another, we would never know. The following week at school rumors circulated about the incident and a consensus emerged as to the identity of the depositor but there never was any final resolution.

I did not pass through Teentown as a choirboy. Our son was about to, an undertaking in some ways akin to stunts like swimming the English Channel. I sought and always found paths of lesser resistance as a schoolboy like sports and drinking.

My cronies and I made much mischief, but never anything like dropping a deuce at the site of a party where we were persona non grata; especially not as mere 8th graders!

Just dawning were the darker implications of my suspicion that our children were growing up in times very different from the fondly recalled ones of my own childhood.

Just because he was the eldest didn't mean that Max was the only one fighting for survival.

Ben too was turning a corner down below in 5th grade and I wonder now if he ever felt like he was going it alone.

He'd always been quieter than his big brother and far more so than his bullhorn father. After showing early signs of becoming an earnest carnivore when he'd sit in his highchair gnawing on pork chop bones, his appetites and diet stagnated.

He had the same kindergarten teacher that broke Max in but this pairing didn't click quite like the first one had. She practically scolded Ben because his small motor skills were slow to develop.

We thought of him as a tough stoic when he racked up most of the brood's stitch count on the occasional trip to the ER. Once he came running in from an after school bike ride around the block with blood gushing from a bite on his upper lip inflicted by a neighbor's dog that he knew well. We'd always had dogs and Ben loved them; he didn't even hold this wound against the biter after he had to endure shots directly in the bitten tissue before the plastic surgeon could sew his mouth back together. Somehow Ben must have realized that the old pooch bit him because she was startled by his sudden approach from behind - if she had known it was good ol' Ben comin' up on her she would have licked, not bitten.

When Max and Ben were in 3rd grade and kindergarten, respectively, we pulled them both from public school in mid-year in favor of a newly opened Christian "academy." It was a move that was misguided and would be reversed soon enough, but in retrospect it may have been particularly ill-timed where Ben was concerned. By 2nd grade he was back in public school with a good teacher, but in 3rd grade he drew a pregnant one who was preoccupied with a squad of noisemakers in her class. Ben was not a troublemaker; indeed, he wasn't much of an attention-getter of any sort. After growing out of his chunky toddler stage he was emerging as a small, quiet kid - all the easier for him to slip through cracks. He was the classic middle child, chronologically equidistant from an older brother and a younger sister. He was absolutely beautiful - pictures of him from his grade school days are all radiant but few of them captured him smiling.

STUBS

By 5th grade Ben was complaining about the textures of foods as we groped for ways to get him to eat something besides bread and candy. Then he started reporting occasional difficulty breathing and general anxiety at bedtime.

When the kids were all small and our authority still went unchallenged bedtime became a cherished ritual for me, and not just because outlasting them meant that we had won another round. As the last one standing I got to lock up the house after a decompressing smoke out on the front porch with the dogs.

Then I'd douse the downstairs lights before climbing the stairs and making the rounds of the bedrooms. It was like each child was reborn to me every night, minus the medical worries of childbirth. There were a couple of sublime moments on even the worst of days when I was alone with our children and the realization that I'd managed to outlast the worst of my personal demons. I had been delivered from 25 years of intermittent blackout to an unforgettable decade plus.

If world peace was out of reach at least there was finally peace in my corner of it; peace that I could stick out my arm and touch; peace that I could bend down and kiss. And I did, every night, before I too fell peacefully asleep with whom it all began.

But then Max got a 3rd floor bedroom when we moved to a bigger house and became more of a boarder.

And Ben; beautiful, quiet Ben suddenly couldn't fall asleep on his own.

When we left his parent/teacher conference in the fall of his 5th grade year Ben's eyes brimmed with tears. His teacher, a popular one at the school who liked to do magic tricks and otherwise perform for his classes, took Ben to task, not so much for misbehavior as inattention and what he saw as laziness.

Belatedly, Chris and I started to consider the possibility of ADD. An unfortunate side effect of my general nostalgia for old ways was that I scoffed at modern maladies as contemporary poppy-cock dreamed up by the pharmaceutical giants to sell more of their potions. The vague stereotype of an ADD kid that I carried around was actually more of an ADHD profile with the emphasis on the H for hyperactivity. Ben had never evidenced hyperactivity in the context of a classroom and outside of school his playful industry and brief attention spans seemed as typical to us of little boys as freckles and frogs.

Chris got some material from her school and we started indexing some of Ben's characteristics against these measuring sticks. I found myself reflecting on things like his tendency to run outside and play baseball, even by himself, as opposed to sitting and watching a game inside with Max and I for more than a batter or two at a time.

Pretty quickly it became obvious what Ben had been up against. So obvious that we felt we'd been failing him almost from the start of his schooldays. How could we have paid so much attention and seen so little?

We went for a consultation as to medication; how much, and of what? It seemed like a pill-popping process of trial and error.

Whatever gains were made in Ben's ability to focus his way through a day of school came at the cost of his emerging personality and seemed also to further suppress an appetite that we were already concerned about. He was at an age when Max had started the growth spurt that fires boys into adolescence and removes them further from the pull of home and family.

I didn't think it any fairer to compare Ben's physical and emotional development to Max's than I'd figured it was to compare Max's to what I remembered about my own. Everyone's entitled to be themselves, right? Still, it was hard not to refer to experience and end up second guessing things we'd done and not done. We often flew by instruments alone and our instruments consisted of hunches, good intentions and prayers. We more or less knew where we wanted to go but it was getting harder and harder to figure out where we were.

As for Emma, she was still wading in the relatively safe single digits; her innocence essentially intact. Her time would come. As a family we were about to attempt the dreaded triple spinner: a high-schooler, middle-schooler and grade-schooler, all at the same time!

Forever and Ever Land

One Sunday in February of 2005 when Emma was eight she and Chris went downtown to see *Peter Pan* at the Civic Center. It was a matinee performance at 1:00 in the afternoon. We usually got home from the 10:00 A.M. service at church around 11:30 and more weeks than not we'd enjoy our variation of a ploughman's lunch - grilled cheese sandwiches, dill pickles and cold milk before scattering to whatever presented on our respective agendas.

I don't know what story Emma heard and talked about that morning in Sunday school and I cannot say that its juxtaposition with the staging of a tale about a magical boy who refused to grow up caused her any measure of confusion. Maybe it needn't have since the handbook of Christendom endorses childlike faith. I do know that she has been in the habit of earnest prayer going back at least that far and that she seems quite intent on growing up. If she was ever fascinated by the flights of Peter or Tinkerbelle or pixie dust, the spell must have broken in short order and been briefer than a pediatric fever. Her faith, on the other hand, seems chronic.

Here is where I'd like to drop hints to you that Emma and her brothers took faith from their old man as surely as they did blue eyes. But bringing them to church has been more along the lines of taking helpers along to wash the car. They see you scrubbing and rinsing, even help out and get a little wet when you turn the spray on them, lightening the mood before everybody drives home together feeling, for at least a while, cleansed and shiny. By the time you get home the world's grime has already started its comeback.

The truth is that Emma, her brothers and their mother are the biggest leaps I've ever taken. Liturgically I give some benefits of doubt, even credence, to articles of my parents' faiths. They were both good and smart people. Their credibility ratings have remained high, even risen, in the years since their passings. It would not have mattered to them whether or not I bought the notion that Enoch lived to be 365 years old but I trust they somehow remain pleased that I ascribe value and power to prayer, and that sometimes there flares in me a spirit that is best described as holy. Like a geyser it rises and subsides.

At about this point in her life Emma was really into country singer Sara Evans; don't ask me how that happened because I don't know. Nothing against country music in general or Sara in particular; it's just that you never know what your kids are gonna bring home with 'em - stray cats, head lice, new bacterial strains, what have you...

We would hear her up in her room belting out the lyrics of *Saints & Angels,* a hit song for Evans back then. Sometimes Emma would sing that song in the car on our way to church. I liked it. We even saw it performed live when Evans came to the Iowa State Fair a couple of summers prior. Whenever Emma sang it her face contorted passionately; she was fully invested, especially the parts about, *love has the grace to save us,* and, *in each other's arms, we become saints and angels...*

If I were gonna hymn my theology in the context of popular, contemporary music I'd probably go with Eric Clapton's *My Father's Eyes* or this line from Sara McLachlan's *Arms of an Angel:* "*...the glorious sadness that brings me to my knees...*"

Emma is the only one of our children whose life fits entirely within the period of my ongoing sobriety. The last time I was drunk Max was a toddler, Ben was an infant and Emma was not yet even a good idea.

Her father used to be a Lost Boy; a disciple of Pan's. She's turned out to be a very good idea indeed; both saintly and angelic.

I used to think I took my family to church. Maybe they were taking me. They make a fine sanctuary.

The Albuquerque Isotopes?!

In keeping with tradition I took my sons to the ballpark on Friday, April 15, 2005 for the Iowa Cubs' first home game of the year. The tickets said *"OPENING DAY"* just beneath 7:05 P.M. It was really a night game but inasmuch as it began before sundown and was anticipated throughout that morning and afternoon, we would not have quibbled the point.

The evening's opponents were the Isotopes from Albuquerque, the Englebert Humperdinks of professional baseball.

Through some bizarre reshuffling of the deck of minor league ball clubs our Triple A team found itself reassigned from the landlocked American Association to the Pacific Coast League, a consortium as far-flung as the Milky Way, stretching all the way from Tacoma to Nashville. It was a twilight zone of team names that included not only the Isotopes but the 51's just up the road in Las Vegas, a nod to the area's association with UFO's. Rod Serling's signature should have been on the league's official baseballs. The further inland the PCL branched the more pedestrian became the teams. Outposts in Omaha and Des Moines were respectively coined the Royals and Cubs in unimaginative deference to their big league affiliations. The Midwestern teams were as far removed from the seaside ones in nomenclature as were Nebraska and Iowa from the coast and its culture. Only the league standings could meaningfully bunch such a disparate collection of barnstormers.

If the boys asked me what Isotopes were I can't imagine how I would have answered so atomically weighty a question. I may have said Isotopes were a brand of baseball gloves and quickly changed the isotopic.

As was our custom at April's first games we did not stay to the bitterly cold end that night. Having met our self-imposed obligation of being there to mark the return of ballplayers to the north, we adjourned early and left the rest of the game uneaten on our plate, a good meal gone cold.

2005 was the last time the three of us went together to the I-Cubs' home opener. I was in the process of being outgrown.

When dads and their boys go to the ballpark there are dynamics at work more subtle than when to pull the infield in and who gets the green light on a 3-0 count. What goes on in the restroom, for instance, more ensures the future of the game than between-inning mascotry and PA orchestrated sing-alongs. There, men of all sizes, shapes and ages mingle and the circle of life is splayed horizontally across a bank of urinals - everybody from a squirt; no, make that a half-pint with his super-hero briefs at his ankles to an aging veteran seasoning his output with tobacco juice spat into the mix like a dash of bitters. It is a more modest variation of the locker room anthropology I remember from boyhood visits to the YMCA. That was the first place where I had to drop inhibitions and underwear in a roomful of naked fellas. The elders padded about like bull elephants with their trunks bobbing. I couldn't imagine something similar sprouting from the denuded bud that was then barely serviceable for me as a urinator valve.

There is a masculine osmosis at work in settings like restrooms beneath the grandstands and locker rooms at the Y that is a vital part of one generation's passing of the torch to the next. I was going to miss it soon enough.

By then Max could more than hold his own in a baseball debate - philosophical or statistical - even as his life shifted its emphasis from sports to the arts. He still valued his extensive card collection as evidenced by his insistence that it remain stored in his room instead of being relegated to the clutter department in the basement. But he was regarding it now more as a relic than as currency in his pocket. His formerly frequent "separations," i.e., reorganization of his holdings by era or team or position had become very occasional. As high school loomed just a year up ahead Max was already beginning to put childish things aside.

Ben however was embarking on a season to remember. His 11 year-old regular little league season was unremarkable, the Raccoon Valley Cubs losing more often than they won. But Ben was chosen to represent them on the league's all-star squad and that's when the season really took off.

STUBS

The boys went on a ten-game tear all the way to the state championship.

Ben singled away at a .500 clip and manned centerfield in a reliable, workmanlike fashion. He did not strike out even once and knocked in the first run of the championship game.

The state tournament was played in exotic Sioux City where Ben and I were roommates for a few days in a hotel that overlooked the Missouri River. But I carry with me an indelible memory from a game very early on the team's tournament trail that feels characteristic of the overall experience of Ben's Little League years.

Ben led off the bottom of the 6th [the last inning of a regulation little league game] with the score tied. He lined a single and continued to second base when the ball bad-hopped past the center fielder. Then he advanced to third on a wild pitch. When one of the team's real standouts, a lanky but morose natural athlete, managed a routine grounder to short Ben crossed the plate with the winning run and immediately detoured up the 1st baseline in search of a celebratory chest bump or embrace or, at minimum, a high-five from his deliverer. Instead he was rebuffed by a pouting teammate unsatisfied by the manner in which he'd won the game for his team.

Ben's chance to cement his spot on a good team dissolved into a reaffirmation of his place at its fringes. He'd always been a classic ragamuffin playing ball in the era of the uniform; a free-range sand-lotter in the age of the batting-caged; a footloose kid with a mitt swimming against a current of fancy gear bags and parents who wore team shirts with their child's name and number on the back.

He would have fit better in the society of the neighborhood where I'd grown up and I imagine that he and I would have played a lot of ball together and been good pals. As it was, I tried to father him without trying to make him a serious ballplayer. What he wanted was someone to play with; not a coach.

During that state tournament in Sioux City the boys whiled away the hours between games by doing what came naturally: playing elevator tag inside the hotel or good old-fashioned whiffleball on the grounds outside above the riverbank. Notwithstanding their official triumphs and trophies, those were the best games I ever saw them play.

Suddenly, or did it just seem that way, instead of buying tickets to take the kids to some event or other I was buying tickets to watch *them* perform! I thought we as parents should have been on some sort of pass list. Don't think me cheap - as much as I loved to watch Ben play ball or Emma play soccer or listen to Max and his choirs sing, I figured admissions should have been rolled into the up front and ongoing fees we paid just to get them involved in the first place. I wanted to say, "our donation is our child…" Instead I'd ante up, take a seat and take it in.

All around us jockeyed for prime photographic vantage points.

There is a brazen narcissism now at large in the land that is spreading unchecked. Sometimes it's mistaken for devoted parenting and it can be caught from cell phones, digital cameras and camcorders the way influenza is contracted on door knobs and toilet seats.

Not every moment is a Kodak. Not every occasion is special. We have become invaders of our own privacies.

Children still have a right to strike out without cameras rolling just like grownups used to be entitled to make undocumented asses of themselves, a now endangered principle from which I profited repeatedly many years ago.

Return to the Scene of the Crime

By June of '05 we musketeers were back in the stands at Wrigley Field. The three of us hit the road upon the end of the school year to see the Cubs do battle with the upstart and nouveau riche Florida Marlins, the franchise that took what had seemed to be our rightful place in the 2003 World Series.

I had come to despise the Marlins who'd only just come into existence as an expansion team in 1993. By the time they were 10 years old they'd won two world championships without first winning so much as a divisional title. Their regular season home games played to crowds commensurate in numbers to those drawn by minor league games in Des Moines. The team and what comparatively few "fans" were truly attached to it were like folks who only buy lottery tickets when the jackpot is sufficiently enormous to interest them. Then they win. And just two years prior they'd stomped on us beggars en route to claiming their prize. We were long-suffering. They weren't long anything.

We had a neighbor then who lived across the street in a retirement community. He'd grown up in Chicago not far from Wrigley Field and used to tell the boys stories about playing hooky from school to park cars on game days. He told us his boyhood address and asked if we'd see what had become of it on one of our trips to Chicago.

This was the one.

We were booked at a modest hotel in Lincoln Park; north of downtown and barely a mile's walk to the ballpark. As we made our way there on the night of Monday, June 13, we realized that we were passing through Jonas' old neighborhood and made the slight detour required to route us past the house where he'd grown up. It was intact but subdivided by then into multiple condominiums, one of which was for rent. The block was working class but, by virtue of its location in the heart of what had become known as Wrigleyville during the ballpark's rise to landmark status, real estate there commanded steep prices that didn't square with the hardscrabble hustlings of Jonas' youth.

When we walked away after, yes, taking some pictures for our neighbor, and resumed our trek to the ballgame, Ben found a $20 bill on the sidewalk. We decided to regard it as Jonas' way of buying us some refreshments at the park in exchange for us checking up on a place that was still, in some ways, home to him.

The cash find was nice but became secondary very shortly to my lucky snag of a BP ball that bounced practically right to me almost as soon as we arrived at the intersection of Waveland and Kenmore. I told the boys that lots of tourists had one Waveland Ave. BP souvenir, but only a true ballhawk could claim two or more.

We seemed to be enjoying a rather lucky day, but, as only they can do, the Cubs broke whatever spell was in the air by getting thrashed 9-1 in that evening's game which we suffered through from the upper deck boxes. The next night they won, 14-0, led by Derrek Lee who was on his way to the best season of his career. We cheered ourselves hoarse from the familiar and familial section of the bleachers which offered asylum from the beer vendors and their unquenchable clientele. In a touch of irony that only the mercenary transience of major league baseball could produce, Lee was our favorite Cub that year, just two years after playing a key role in the championship run of the hated Marlins.

Between Two Lovers

In August it was Chris and I, just the two of us, on another of our, "you do your thing, I'll do mine," getaways in celebration of our 16th anniversary.

As usual, by day she shopped and I ballgamed. At night we dated. On Saturday the 13th we saw *Wicked* from Row Z on the main floor of the Oriental Theatre in the evening after I enjoyed a Cub/Cardinal clash from a club box seat only six rows off the field.

Tough as even bad seats at Cub games were getting to come by, I'd learned that you can always get good last minute walk-up tickets if you only need one or two. Choice chairs reserved for insiders that would otherwise go unused get put back in inventory on game days. The Cubs had won the previous day's game and lost this one in keeping with their slightly sub-.500 record that season which had them mired nearly 20 games in arrears of their front-running rivals. That two-game snapshot was also in keeping with their historical penchant for rewarding allegiance with more pain than pleasure.

So having spent consecutive afternoons with my mistress I gave that evening to a truer love and we watched Ana Gasteyer in the role of the green with envy witch, a further cry from her SNL sketches than we would have imagined her capable of. Our evening together was the highlight of that trip. A day at Wrigley could never feel blasé but was becoming as familiar as a favorite pair of shoes or trousers. The night on the town was like stepping out in a new suit with a pretty girl on my arm.

Each Cub game was essentially the next act in a long-running comedy/tragedy with the ultimate outcome predetermined. But *Wicked* was a variation; an oft-told story from a different perspective. If the Cubs had me asking, "So what else is new?" *Wicked* was the answer.

The occasional days that Chris and I stole and kept for ourselves always included comparisons of notes about our children. And those sessions were always a mix of prideful "look what we did" and exasperated "what are we gonna do?" I was past 50 now; Chris was only just closing in on 40. She was early in her career as a teacher and my days at the saloon were feeling numbered. Before I took her home we shared a sense that things were good but also in flux and up for grabs.

Extreme Commuter

There was just one more thing I had to tend to in Chicago that summer before Chris and the kids went back to school. After I ran her home from our anniversary date I dashed back a couple weeks later when the Cubs retired Ryne Sandberg's jersey #23 in pre-game ceremonies on August 28th.

They were passing out commemorative baseball cards at the turnstiles that day and I was happily surprised that a fair number of folks simply discarded their token of admission as though it were nothing more than a coupon for a buck off at the dry cleaners or a flier under the windshield wiper with instructions on how to live. Like a kid harvesting candy tossed from parade floats I gathered up a dozen or so besides the one I was handed in exchange for my ticket.

Sandberg had just been inducted into baseball's Hall of Fame about a month earlier and he rose to that occasion with a rather impassioned speech that had seemed out of character. In his playing days he'd been steadily productive and occasionally spectacular but always taciturn. He'd appeared to be doing something he was naturally good at [to the point of being tagged with the nickname of "Kid Natural" early in his career, but he was so bland off the field it didn't stick] but could take or leave. Indeed, his career was marked by a false, premature retirement in 1994 from which he returned in 1996 to play two more years before hanging 'em up for good after the 1997 season. His Cooperstown address made clear what the game and his career and the fans had always meant to him. It felt to me at the time like a rallying breeze; the sort of proclamation that made me feel less of a dope for giving such a damn about a team that gave back so little that was tangible.

In lieu of World Series appearances I'd salvaged what I could from fleets of sunken hopes.

One compartment of the three in the drawer otherwise reserved for my under things has been overrun with memento baseballs. Out in the garage is a restored chair that once was bolted in place at my favorite ballpark. I have a square tin box that's made to look like that place. When I open it to deposit, for instance, a Ryne Sandberg Jersey Retirement Day baseball card for safekeeping, "Take Me Out to the Ballgame" starts to play. And then there are the flags.

My wife has an uncle who's both a craftsman and something of a flea marketeer. Some years ago she was visiting him and her aunt and discovered him in his shop restoring a rather grand, commercial/institutional grade flagpole. It was hexagonal and gradually tapered from its base to the golden ball that topped it off. We lived then in a three-story gabled home [I liked to think of it as The House of Raised Eyebrows] draped by a shawl of vines and shaded by three old burr oak trees. Chris bought the pole for me as a Father's Day gift. Her uncle painted it white and then installed it like a giant cribbage peg in our front yard. It rose up perhaps 25 feet among the oaks and I set about collecting a wardrobe to adorn it.

I got a nice 4′x6′ American flag that had flown over the Capitol building in Des Moines for the 4th of July and Memorial Day. I had Iowa Hawkeye and Chicago Bear flags for football season. There was a skull & crossbones for Halloween and a cross for Christmas and Easter. And there was a W for baseball season.

A long time before me the custom developed in Chicago of signaling whether the Cubs had won or lost that afternoon's home game by flying the appropriate flag atop the pole that was atop the scoreboard at the ballpark. There was a blue flag with a white L and a white flag with a blue W and they were visible far and wide to commuters making their ways home from work on the trains.

Now Cub fans everywhere have their very own W flags and the ritual is re-enacted from sea to shining sea. You don't see too many of the L flags, though I did actually buy one once on E-bay that had flown [so often that it was frayed at its ends] over THE scoreboard. Unable to obtain an equally authentic W flag I got my own commercial version and started my own custom. Each year on Opening Day I'd run it up the pole and leave it there throughout the long season. When the Cubs lost it was simply lowered to half-staff. Not until we prepared to move several seasons later did I learn that the old widow who lived across the street had first thought the W represented a sort of family crest and that every time it was lowered marked the death of someone from our extended family.

Defeat was hard, yes, but not on that scale. Baseball teams are reborn 162 times per summer.

No Admittance

On Saturday October 22, 2005, not long after baseball's regular season ended with the Cubs again falling by the wayside, I was dispatched to deliver Max to Indianola, a small college town about 20 miles south of Des Moines where he was to audition for the Iowa high school All-State Chorus. He was 14 and had been living the life of a timid freshman for all of a month.

We drove along, me groping for advice to dispense, Max politely refraining from saying, "shut up and drive." What could I tell him? Not only did I know nothing of music, he'd repeatedly shown himself to be more poised than me. I was doing all I could by giving him a ride.

It was deep autumn and the Iowa countryside was flying its colors. My gaze flickered from the road to the bright roadside vistas to the kid riding quietly alongside me. Who was he? Where had he come from? Already he'd earned more respect from me than I accord most adults I know. Generally speaking I prefer most dogs to most folks. But Max, besides all of the other ways he affected me, was intriguing. He seemed to have come equipped with capabilities that were activated by decisions he made like putting batteries in a gadget. His musical knacks could be explained as both provident and para-genetic; as soon as they began to emerge I heard my mother in him - the one-time college chorister/grandmother who died the year before Max was born. But his self-confidence and work ethic were what really trademarked him in my estimation. He was my son but he little resembled me in his most distinctive characteristics.

When we got to Indianola and found the high school hosting the auditions I noticed that most kids were either part of a group or in the company of parents and teachers. But Max insisted on going it alone. When he got out of the car and walked away he couldn't see the admiring stare that followed him. I wondered if he could feel it.

That afternoon I was at home watching the Iowa football game, a tough double overtime loss to Michigan, when a phone call came telling us that our kid was an all-stater. Later we got a bumper sticker that said the same thing which we never peeled. On November 19, when the Hawkeyes pounded their archrival Minnesota on the gridiron, I was at the Iowa All-State Music Festival.

It's a tough ticket but I had a connection.

Um-Ya-Ya

The St. Olaf choir was touring in January, 2006 and stopped in Des Moines on Saturday the 28th to sing at a church across from the campus of Drake. Max was out of town with a choral group from school but Chris and I plunked down 20 bucks apiece to hear a program that made the case for things unseen better than the televangelists ever have or will. Heaven heard is more compelling than hell forewarned.

The son of a cousin of mine was a member of that year's edition of the choir. He was just the latest in a choral line that's drawn through our family all the way back to my mother's time at the Norwegian Lutheran bastion on the hill in Northfield, Minnesota in the days of F. Melius Christiansen himself. Haven't heard of him? That's what you think. Nowadays it's commonplace for college, and even high school ensembles to tour overseas. In fact, Max would be going to Europe later that year with the Heartland Youth Choir to sing at Mozart's 250th birthday party. But when Maestro Melius steamed across to the old country with the St. Olaf band in 1906 it was the collegiate musical equivalent of Lindbergh's crossing of the Atlantic.

Listening to the Ole choir at this stage was almost a séance for me. I felt I was the medium that channeled between my songstress mother and a grandson she'd just missed in the generational comings and goings. St. Olaf wasn't the place for me. I served my freshman year there but my loud voice has never blended very well with others. I did lots of howling at the moon but no singing whatsoever before finishing my degree down south at the University of Iowa.

Now I started to wonder if maybe Max might be St. Olaf bound. That concert was a potion of mysterious spirituality and pragmatic assessment of a prospective college; sort of like visiting an admissions counselor with a darkened office and a crystal ball and tarot cards.

I left feeling almost as though we'd gotten four tickets for the price of two. Talking briefly with my second cousin afterwards was an encapsulation of the family reunion we'd gathered for in Minnesota a few summers earlier. All in all the evening was both time and money well spent. It gave me a fuller answer to the questions I'd mulled while driving Max to his all-state audition that fall - who was he and where had he come from? And it gave me too perhaps a better sense of where I fit in the whole grand, truly grand, scheme of things.

A Pride of Wellmen

In March the five of us cashed in another theatrical Christmas gift from Chris' dad when we went together to see *The Lion King*. Chris and Max had seen the show on Broadway when she chaperoned his choir's trip to New York City in 2004 that culminated with the group's performance at Carnegie Hall.

They touted the show enthusiastically to the rest of us and we ended up seated near the aisle where many in the cast made their entrances right through the audience and up onto the stage. It was a momentary safari. I absorbed the evening in character as the Mufasa to our pride [and joys]. Separated from me; no, make that connected, by three seats worth of cubs was our Nala, the lioness that every family needs. Maybe you've noticed - it's a jungle out there! I looked to my right in the dark, at the four pairs of eyes riveted on the stage and suppressed a territorial roar.

Please Excuse

When I was in middle school it was still called junior high. There were other more substantive differences between those times and these. One concerns the starting times for World Series games. They used to all be matinees. This was problematic for schoolboy baseball fans, but no more so than a fence running through the route of a favorite shortcut. That is to say we found a way.

In the fall of 1968 the Cardinals and Tigers hooked up in a true October classic. Bob Gibson, Lou Brock, Denny McClain and Mickey Lolich. It would have been a shame to miss it and so, in an adolescent spirit of morally obliged civil disobedience I took it upon myself to tunnel us out of school. I forged a batch of parental notes excusing me and my pals for an unlikely spate of appointments with doctors and dentists of various specialties in a compressed timeline. The guiding principle was to scribble at what I reasoned was an adult level of illegibility.

It was an all too easily followed paper trail but by the time it led the school's disciplinary bloodhounds to me the series was over and our mission was accomplished. We had a lone confederate on the outside, a buddy's complicit mother who, while maintaining plausible deniability as to the means of our mid-day dismissals was nevertheless happy to grant us asylum in her home complete with TV and sumptuous feeds she catered in from McDonalds.

Had the games then been nocturnal and more easily accessed I'm not sure we'd have found them quite as irresistible.

Throughout my boyhood getting updates on World Series games in progress while at school was tantamount to intelligence gathering. That element of espionage far surpassed the freedom of information that marks the ESPN age.

To their credit, the Iowa Cubs scheduled their 2006 home opener as a day game. Why not? As previously noted, the weather was usually not baseball-worthy by the time the season started in the upper Midwest and nighttime openers usually drew a large but early-departing crowd.

The date was April 6, a Thursday; a school day. I saw an Opening Day opening. By way of re-enacting a crude facsimile of my junior high school skipping caper I decided to spring Ben and a carful of classmates from school that afternoon for a field trip to the ballpark. They were 7th graders at the same school I'd played hooky from in 1968. Of course, it wasn't the World Series and being sprung from class by dad wasn't the same as forging his signature to a note about a bogus appointment with an herbal healer. Still, it was a ballgame trumping school and that counted for something. The notes written this time were legit and forthright about the reason for the early dismissals. I picked the boys up at school and it was all I could do as we drove downtown not to join in with their rowdy pre-game warm-ups. It was baseball season and we, I mean they, were out of the classroom and on the way to a ballpark.

We sat just a couple rows removed from the field, mere feet away from the I-Cubs' bullpen. While my charges clamored for the autograph of that year's designated phenom-on-the-come, Felix Pie [pronounced like the abbreviation for public address], I struck up an amiable, it's opening day and life is good chat with one of the team's pitchers, Bobby Brownlie. Brownlie had signed with the Cub organization a couple of years earlier as a high draft pick. He'd come into the fold highly touted and managed to reach Triple A, but his rise through the ranks had hardly been meteoric. His friendly chatter twanged slightly southern and I made a note to myself that he should be my personal favorite that summer; my own dark horse stable mate of the can't miss thoroughbred, Pie.

Sure enough, my new pal was summoned to protect a lead in the 6th inning. He gave up four runs and was charged with the first loss of a season ledger that would end up at 3-14 in service to two teams. By the time the boys were out of school for the summer his career had u-turned back to Double A.

Nice guys don't necessarily finish last but they sure as hell don't always win.

It was a good day for us if not for Brownlie and his teammates [they dropped the opener, 8-4] and I hope an educational experience for my young companions. We learned about regression towards the mean and the law of large numbers when it was explained that statistics compiled from the 1st game of a 144 game schedule are generally useless as predictors of final averages. The triple digit ERA's and .750 batting averages and the extrapolations they yield are misleading but fun.

I also had a great history lesson to share with the students if time had permitted.

The 2006 season marked the centennial of the best ball club that ever took the field in Des Moines. The Des Moines Champions were the renamed encore of the 1905 Western League pennant winners, the Prohibitionists. The Champions went 97-50 and finished 23 games clear of 2nd place Lincoln [NE]. They were managed by an Irish immigrant named Dirty Jack Doyle and their pitching staff included the promising Eddie Cicotte who tossed a no-hitter that year against Omaha. Cicotte later rose [?] to infamy as the ace/ringleader of the 1917 Chicago Black Sox.

We'll never know what the fellas missed that afternoon at school.

An Old Boss of Mine

When I was a college student at the University of Iowa in the mid-1970's I had occasion to work on the stage crew at Hancher Auditorium for a show by a then ascendant rock star named Bruce Springsteen. Though I enjoyed it in ways that only collegians get to enjoy things, the experience was mostly lost on me at the time. I had never heard of Springsteen until the weeks leading to his Iowa City concert so there was no sense for me then of being in on the emergence of something lasting in the transient universe of rock stardom. These were the bibulous days of literally higher learning and the routines of them were interrupted occasionally by on-campus concerts. I figured this was just one more of those. I little knew that I had an up-close view to the unveiling of a phenomenon.

Springsteen's breakthrough album *Born to Run,* just then releasing, became the soundtrack to my last year in school. Decades later, when making solo trips to Chicago as a Cub pilgrim, I'd still make a point of blaring the *Jungleland* track and singing along while glancing off the highway shoulders lost in some misunderstood youth angst fantasy.

But that 1975 concert was the only time I saw Springsteen live until June 10, 2006 when he came to Wells Fargo Arena in Des Moines.

Chris took me. We weren't exactly backstage, but our seats @ $86 per weren't bad. The big arena with a capacity of over 15,000 was pared down to accommodate a crowd of only 5,000 or so, about twice the size of the full house in Iowa City 30 years prior. The Des Moines appearance was a stop on a tour billed as The Seeger Sessions. It was Springsteen's tributary nod to folk singer/songwriter Pete Seeger.

The songs were different but the same. Prayers, really, set to music. Pleases and thank yous sung at heaven.

Since I helped roll speakers off the truck in 1975 Bruce Springsteen had become an iconic celebrity. Me, I got out of show business and took a long break from purposeful, constructive living. By the time our paths crossed again we'd found our separate ways to the same place: a house full of people listening to our music and applauding.

We were both bachelors until the age of 35 before marrying younger and we both have three kids; two sons and a daughter apiece.

Despite all that we have in common we lost touch with one another over the years. It was good to see him again after so long; almost like catching up with an old college chum.

The Wicked Witch & the North Side

A month later me and my deputies were off to see the wizard.

Our weekend in Oz started off with *Wicked* back at the Oriental Theatre on West Randolph; the same place where Chris and I had seen it the previous summer.

Max enjoyed it on a different level than either Ben or I did; he was about to start his sophomore year at the same high school I'd attended and planned to audition for the fall musical there, *Grease*. Not only had I not appeared in any formally staged dramatics at dear old Roosevelt, I didn't attend any of the productions either. In fact, I couldn't have told Max what any of them were during my years there if he'd thought to ask me. But I was nevertheless excited at the prospect of his theatrical debut. He'd landed a role in the previous spring play, but *Grease* would be his first musical so I think he took in *Wicked* that weekend the way he may have watched ballgames as a little boy; that is, imagining himself on the field and in the game. His time was coming.

In keeping with the general mix of our lives, Friday night at the theatre was followed by two sessions at Wrigley Field watching our surrogates joust with the hated Mets from New York.

On Saturday July 15th we worked up a good sweat during our now customary pre-game round of catch and ballhawking on Waveland Avenue. It was hot that weekend in Chicago, temperatures in the 90's. Our seats were cheap ones in the upper deck but at least they were shaded by the rim of the ballpark and in the path of the prevailing air currents.

The Cubs had lost 20 games more than they'd won to that point of that season and the Mets' record was more or less the inverse of ours so the games were tension-free.

We chuckled our way through a 9-3 win that was pitched by Carlos Zambrano. As an added bonus he stole a base, a rare tactic for a pitcher to employ at the major league level. And of course he did it in his own inimitable way, finally dropping down into an awkward slide at the last instant that looked like it might have broken his ankle. Ah, Carlos!

It didn't occur to me then but does now that the boys sitting next to me that day at Wrigley Field had done more growing up than he in the several years since they'd gotten his autograph back home at Sec Taylor Field in Des Moines.

Sunday's game started at the odd time of 5:00 by order of ESPN. That was not its only unusual aspect. In the top of the 6th inning the Cubs took the field with a 5-2 lead. Their pitcher, a rookie southpaw named Sean Marshall, looked good and had even contributed a home run in support of his own cause.

As twilight enveloped the scene an episode of *The Twilight Zone* ensued.

By the time the Mets were finished more than half an hour later they'd scored 11 runs. Their onslaught included not one but two grand slams, one of them by our old nemesis, Carlos Beltran. It was the biggest inning in the Mets' history and the only time in the Cubs' that they'd surrendered two slams before they could get three outs.

Again in the upper reaches of the upper deck, we sat near some apparently transplanted New Yorkers and we siphoned our own measure of rejoicing from their celebratory histrionics. What the hell, the season was already as lost as that particular piece of it but we were in a good place in good company. We might even have said at the time, in so many words, "it's all good."

Sweet Babies By Any Names

In August Chris and I went with some friends to see James Taylor perform as one of the grandstand shows at that summer's edition of the Iowa State Fair. It was Friday the 11th, the day before our wedding anniversary.

Taylor's gentle tunes blended perfectly with the gradually deepening shades of a brilliant sunset and a reflective mood was struck that lingered after the encore and the crowd had faded away.

The next day our marriage turned 17. By the mysterious calculus of romance our two lives had merged into one before shooting off into three others.

Max was then 15, Ben 12 and Emma nine. Our simmering stew was about to boil.

Shifting Gears

About six weeks later we completed our concert hat trick for the year when we went to see The Who at Wells Fargo Arena on September 26, the same venue where we'd launched that summer at the Springsteen show back in June.

I had never seen the band live and listening to them at this point of my life was like setting a former lifestyle to music.

I was one week away from divesting myself of a business, the pub, that had been in our family for a quarter century; one which had provided a good living but was an outgrowth of a way of life gone bad.

Opened by my older brother before passing into my ownership, Wellman's Pub had run its course in my life. 12 years after taking my last drink [fittingly, at Wellman's] I stopped selling them too.

I was running myself off the road of least resistance and taking passengers with me in search of a new path. It felt reckless but refreshing. My life was way behind schedule. When I stopped drinking I was 40 chronologically, 50+ physically and 15 emotionally, the age when I took my first drink.

There was a chronic throb inside that had once been dream-like and now threatened to go with me to my deathbed and haunt me there in the form of a duty not done. Longing always to write and in the face of some evidence that I was intended for it, I'd drifted instead into a rather aimless lifestyle.

And why? Because there was no guarantee that success lay waiting to catch me somewhere beyond a leap of openly declared ambition.

I felt like a lip-synching front man for a band with great musicians behind me. An *Eminence Front* you could say.

Time Out

I was at a point of wondering what they must think of me.

When I'd been really bringing home lots of bacon they were too young to notice or care. Even though my work could be exhausting and was honorable in that sense, it hadn't been something that satisfied me on many levels other than the ephemeral ones that ready cash taps into. The kids could see that I was at loose ends, a circumstance with both spiritual and practical implications for all of us.

Daring to try something long dreamed of could almost be spun to sound brave but it began to feel desperate; like crawling onto the roof to put off, but not escape, rising waters. My solution was to write tenderly about tough times; to further expose my kids to the harder truths about their father. They need never have known about my drinking days. By the time they ended Max was two, Ben an infant and Emma had not yet come to be. I might have kept the secret whether or not others would have here in the town where most of it happened and we still live. But in some subliminal way I guess I must have wanted them to know. If being drunk had been my greatest shame, getting sober was my biggest trophy. And that turnaround greatly informed what passed for my faith; on that level I thought it important to share. If I passed to my kids the gene that made alcohol an allergen then should I not tell them so? Their lives had helped saved mine; all the things I imagined I'd done for them were really just by way of repayment. By the time I'm done I expect we'll all be square.

Showtime!

I n November of that year, a month after I'd disentangled myself from the pub and anything that hinted at long-term security, Roosevelt High School staged its production of *Grease*.

Max drew the role of Teen Angel. Besides a few walk-ons as part of the chorus he had one big number, a solo called *Beauty School Dropout*. It was a gaudy number in the spotlight descending a flight of stairs decked out in white tux and tails.

His kindergarten pal David played the lead role of Danny Zuko.

When David and Max palled up on the playground it brought together whole families. Max was the eldest at our house; David was the youngest of three in his and his parents were devout camcordians, but we found ample common ground otherwise on which to pitch tents of friendship.

When the boys were in 3rd grade their fathers enrolled them in a basketball clinic over the winter holiday break from school. It was clear watching them clank layups off the support poles behind the baskets that this was not their niche. The next spring the old men co-coached a soccer team without knowing the rules of the game. It was good exercise for their sons.

As the years ticked by it became obvious that these two would not someday form the battery at Roosevelt that Bob Feller and Nile Kinnick had been in their high school days.

But now here they were as sophomores standing at center stage while their parents sat together in rapt disbelief just a few rows away.

Whatever consideration I'd given to the narrowing gap between me and Max gave way to the realization that I'd been caught in certain areas and passed in some others.

Even past fifty I was still able to whip Max on the golf course or in a driveway game of one-on-one, but he was a formidable debater now when it came to baseball and, away from the athletic arena, it was becoming a mismatch in his favor.

He could sing and even dance a little now. He played trumpet and piano. Not only was he bright, he studied. He was better with people than I and brimmed with a self-confidence that amazed me.

But best of all, we were not in competition; we were teammates. Or maybe I was the coach. It was hard to say. I had no more to do with most of the things I was starting to see that he was any more than a football coach makes a player able to run fast or a manager enables a pitcher to throw a fastball that hums.

I was simply glad and fortunate that we shared space and time together.

Check, Check, Testing 1,2,3...

There are two types of fathers in the world: those who insist their children, sons in particular, follow in their footsteps and those who pray they do not. I'm in the latter group.

By the time we took Max to see Harry Connick perform at Stephens Auditorium in Ames on the campus of Iowa State University in April of 2007 it was clear that he was more of a crooner himself than a slugger.

The month before Max spent a weekend in a local studio recording a CD. It consisted of five cover tunes. His collaborators were all friends ranging in age from his own to a graduate music student who served as an accompanist for the Heartland Youth Choir Max had been part of since 7th grade.

Quite apart from the musical expression that was the focus and final product, the project became a great experience and exercise for him in other areas. He learned a lot about recording technology, budgeting, marketing and production.

Since he was still a few months shy of getting his first driver's license the title of the CD, "Gimme the Keys" seemed a good hint as to where he was in terms of all phases of his development.

All the ballgames over the years were primarily in the spirit of sharing my time and interests with my kids. As noted early on, there were surely some secret fatherly fantasies that my sons might grow into the battery that led the Cubs back to glory. But realistically I'd always known that dads have better shots of making baseball fans than they do of making ballplayers. I wanted somebody to go to ballgames with more than I wanted someone to coach.

Max is a fan of both baseball and his dad and I am a fan of his. But we don't always agree on what's in the best interests of the Cubs.

It occurred to me at the Connick show that Chris and I were there strictly to be entertained. Max, in addition to that purpose, was watching and listening in the same spirit small boys of my generation had regarded Mickey Mantle and Willie Mays. He wanted to emulate as well as be entertained.

He has a better shot at Connick than I ever had at Mantle or Mays.

On (Re)assignment

In the spring of 2007 I attached myself to a blog for Cub fans called *The Cub Reporter*. I prevailed upon the Iowa Cubs to grant me a media credential that I might cover and report on the team from a firsthand perspective for the benefit of fans of the parent team who might care to know what was going on at the upper reaches of the organization's farm system. I was able to arrange occasional access to players for interviews, [including Angel Guzman and Felix Pie who we'd seen play in Chicago at the All-Star Futures game in 2003] and discovered that they generally had nothing of interest to say to strangers wielding notepads and recorders.

I also started doing occasional freelance concert reviews for *The Des Moines Register*. In April it was Peter Frampton at a local casino. In May it was The Killers at an old ballroom where my senior prom had been held. Later would be John Mayer at Wells Fargo Arena and Stephen Stills at the historic Hoyt Sherman Place.

Over the Memorial Day weekend, mere days away from the release event he'd planned for the CD, I drove Max and his friend Patrick to Chicago to see the Cubs play the Florida Marlins. It would be a nice breather between post-production detailing and his coming out party as a recording artist.

Patrick was a talented musician in his own right and had participated in the project as a guitarist and backup vocalist. He and Max first met as Little League teammates and I coached them one year when Patrick was a pudgy catcher I imaginatively nicknamed Yogi and Max was a scatter-gun pitcher who frequently sent Yogi scurrying to the backstop in pursuit of errant fastballs.

Always a quiet kid, Patrick seemed most at ease with himself when he was on stage performing. He had taught himself well on guitar and struck me as least conscious of himself when he was singing for an audience.

Their musical tastes were diverging by then, at least in terms of what they chose to perform. Max was more of a front man jazz vocalist in the style of Sinatra, Connick and Michael Buble [if you can picture that in a 15 year-old] and Patrick tended towards self-accompanied folksy rock a la Jack Johnson.

Besides the CD recording sessions they sang together in their high school's chamber choir and show choir.

We all sang the blues on this whirlwind trip. The Marlins beat the Cubs in a forgettable Memorial Day game.

Feelin' Good

I parlayed the meager proceeds from one of my freelance assignments into two tickets to see Michael Buble at the Auditorium Theatre on July 23, 2007 in Chicago and gave them to Chris and Max for a trip together in celebration of their July birthdays.

She was turning 41 that month. He turned 17.

She felt like all she'd given him was hay fever and acne. But I knew that more importantly he'd also acquired much of his temperament from his mother.

Still evident in Max as an emerging young man was the little boy that stood in his front yard on Harwood Drive and smiled and waved at passing strangers. Even when people failed or disappointed him in some way, he was gentle and forgiving in his dealings with them.

When music teachers at school we reasonably assumed would be mentors instead turned out to be impediments it was Max who found ways around them and kept his parents from becoming squeaky wheels.

I have always been touched by their relationship with one another. Sometimes he demonstrates his feelings for his mother in ways that I wish I did towards my wife.

On their trip together, during the concert, Max told his mom that someday he wanted to play to an audience like they were part of that evening with a big band behind him like the one that backed Buble.

He wasn't exactly revealing a secret. It was more of an update on the prediction he'd made as a squirt when he got nose to nose with Diana Ross singing on TV from the Super Bowl and said, "Someday…"

The longer any of us can preserve the personal prophecies we make as four year-olds the better. Usually they are like bubbles we blow through the wand of life that soon pop. But not always.

Go Cubeyes!

During the spring and summer of 2007 a long-held but still vague notion of writing a book about the neighborhood where I grew up began taking shape. I shared some of my ideas with other people for the first time. Finding encouragement there I put a rough outline and production schedule down on paper. A fuzzy fantasy began stirring to life.

When we went to Chicago over the Labor Day weekend for the twin purposes of seeing the Iowa Hawkeyes open their football season at Soldier Field against Northern Illinois and watching the Cubs close in on a division pennant at Wrigley Field versus the Astros, I was set to begin in earnest. The plan was that when Chris and the kids started back to school I would devote at least the mornings during the week to working on the book manuscript. Afternoons were reserved for laundry, taxiing and other domestic humdrum.

I tried to think of myself as both the taskmaster making assignments and the student carrying them out. If I stayed faithful to the formula enough pages would pile up over the year's course to give me a good sense of whether or not I was onto something.

I had come to a crisis of faith. It was not a question of whether or not I believed that a beleaguered Noah somehow got all the animals on an ark and from there to high ground. It didn't matter that I was convinced God was as dismayed as I about the contamination of worship by politics. My personal theological hunch that anyone who loves and/or is loved by anyone else is thereby saved was irrelevant to the issue at hand which was, very simply: did God have a more specific purpose for me and was I serving it?

It can be hard to divide what we want to believe from what we truly do.

I was convinced that none of us arrives for the express purpose of misery. In my own case, it had been neither God's intention nor my own that the promise of my early years be dissolved in cocktails between the ages of 15 and 40.

As we inched along in Lake Shore Drive traffic on the morning of September 1, 2007, I was feeling on the verge of something. It might have been overdue. It might have been a mistake. But life was changing and that alone had an excitement about it that was energizing.

It was a beautiful day and as we drew within a mile or so of Soldier Field on our way into town we noticed a sea of black and gold superimposed against the magnificent backdrop of Lake Michigan.

It was our people.

I was driving but we were at a standstill in gridlock. I told the boys to hop out of the car and I did the same as I ordered Chris into the pilot's seat. The three of us decided to bypass the downtown hotel check-in and jump straight into the football season.

We stepped over a guard rail and made our way down an

embankment into the midst of the swarm of Iowans decked out like bumblebees that was massing in Chicago.

We'd traded a vehicular impasse for a human one but we made our way through it like small particles slipping through a big clog. Eventually we sweated out the late summer weather and an unexpectedly narrow Iowa victory from the steep slopes of Soldier Field's upper deck.

The Hawkeyes won 16-3, but the game was as boring as I expect football in summer weather to be. The greater drama was keeping tabs on the Cub game on the northside by radio. They eked out a 4-3 win over the Astros to maintain their precarious hold on 1st place as the baseball season turned into its homestretch.

That night we all reassembled for dinner at a sidewalk café along South Michigan Avenue before sampling the Chicago Jazz Festival across the street in Millenium Park. The hot summer day had cooled into a jazzy sort of city evening that felt very promising. I was feeling hip and in my element inasmuch as I was about to become a self-proclaimed author.

We topped off a first-rate day and night with ice cream cones which we lapped up while strolling along a great metropolitan boulevard strewn with the mingled Chicago street people and rural Iowans on a weekend holiday. There was a stark visual contrast that was overridden by a sense that we were all in something together and were all going to be alright.

It must have been the music. It'll do that to you. That and ice cream.

The next day the usual 3/5 of the family was at Wrigley to watch firsthand as the Cubs pulled out a dramatic 6-5 victory when Derrek Lee hit a two-run homer in the bottom of the 8th.

Having exhorted both the Hawks and Cubs to victories in the space of less than 24 hours in a city that exhausts at even a pedestrian's pace we sporting types fell back in retreat to our downtown hotel and feigned interest in the fruits of Chris and Emma's two-day shopping spree.

Bright and early the next morning we headed for home. Each of us had assignments waiting.

Halleleujah!

By the time Chris and I went to see the Des Moines symphony perform Handel's *Messiah* at the Civic Center on December 1, 2007, I was clipping along at a steady pace on my manuscript. There was a story gestating inside of me and watching it form on my computer screen was like seeing fetal growth on an ultrasound. I experienced all the excitement and apprehension of pregnancy. It was going to be beautiful! It was going to be defected! It was moving! I can't feel anything! Everyone will love it! No one will care!

For all the emotional highs and lows inherent in the process, I'm sure the night of Handel was a peak. The Halleleujah

Chorus is a convincing argument on God's behalf; one of those rare wonders that elicits exhilaration and humility simultaneously.

One of Max's peer mentors, Ben, was playing that night in the violin section despite that he had only just graduated from high school the previous spring. By then he was already a veteran symphony performer and an accomplished pianist and classical guitarist as well. He too had collaborated on Max's CD and played keyboard on gigs with Max throughout the year he took off from school to decide on an instrumental preference before enrolling at Indiana University's prestigious Jacobs School of Music.

Christmas was coming, the goose was getting fat.

This would have been the day that we brought home our Christmas tree since it was the first Saturday in December.

Ever since the kids were small we've been in the habit of going out to a tree farm near Cumming, Iowa on the Saturday before Thanksgiving, a traditional Opening Day of another sort. There we browse through the aisles of the pine groves and finally settle on a Douglas Fir to tag as ours. Their needles are short and soft; good for ornament-hanging and easy on the fingertips. A couple of Saturdays later, back we come to lash the tree to the top of the car and bring it home for trimming.

The tree farm operation has enough Currier & Ives working to enable overlooking its rather robust commerciality.

There's a warming house with an electric train up and running. Santa's always there in a La-Z-Boy taking orders. Cheaply priced popcorn, hot chocolate & peppermint sticks occupy us kids while we wait for a crack at Santa and the grownups stand in line to pay for the holiday centerpiece.

Just a ways up the exit road is a "farmhouse" stocked with "bargains" to accent the greening of the home.

Outside a farm dog roams his Shangri-la and a few prop horses panhandle for scrub brush offered them through fence rails by elfin children with all sorts of yuletide visions already dancing in their heads. There's a stack of hay bales for squirts to cavort on, weather permitting.

The kids have sprouted from sprigs to young trees in their own rights since we started this custom and become harder to lose in the maze of quilled green cones than they were when we first came here.

Some years on one or both days of the ritual a gentle snow even fell. Occasionally an overhead hawk screeches attention to itself. At the eastern boundary of the tannenbaum orchard a stand of pines way too tall for indoor duty is posted as a windbreak. They all bend slightly to the north, even when the air is calm, like a halleleujah chorus line.

It is a place we always go, and a thing we always do, together.

Which Way Out of Hannah, Montana?

On Groundhog Day, 2008 I took Emma to see something called *Hanna Montana: The Movie*. According to the stubs, our tickets cost $15.00 each. The *Star Wars* stubs from 11 years earlier [almost to the day; February 1, 1997] when I almost went to jail and left five year-old Max to hitchhike home had been a bargain @ $4 apiece.

Remembering this outing reminds me that I don't do much alone with Emma, just her and me. When she was a little girl I took her to a daddy/daughter dance one Valentine's Day. I don't know exactly when that was because there weren't hard tickets issued. We got dressed up for a night out together - just the two of us. We waltzed without her feet ever touching the floor. Mine did the footwork for both of us while I held her aloft, [like I did a few years later so she could get a glimpse of Raven Somebody at the Iowa State Fair] but I probably didn't feel them much. She was beautiful. She still is, but differently. Then her beauty was ours alone. Time passes and it attracts others, which is fine; it is after all the nature of things - you just hope that you lose your daughter one day to someone who's maybe a better man than you but loves her even half as much.

Ten days from now she becomes a teenager. I hope I can waltz her through the narrows of Hannah Montana and the like to emerge in young adulthood as her authentic self and not a store-bought impersonation of a Disney product carved into the bark of her self-image.

The feelings a man has for his daughter are his love for her mother purified.

Paper-clipped to the Hannah Montana receipts were small stubs from two other movies: *Miracle* and *The Rookie.*

The latter we attended on March 29, 2002. Max would have been 10; Ben, eight.

The date would have been just before baseball renewed, always a morale booster for me and, by extension, the boys too.

The Rookie was the improbable but basically true story of a school teacher/baseball coach with a bum shoulder who makes a diamond-in-the-rough rise to the major leagues for a brief stint as a flame-throwing relief pitcher.

At that point in his young life Max must have been feeling some real ambivalence about baseball. He'd declined that year to go to the little league tryouts for the "majors" division; he lacked confidence in his abilities. That is the only time I have *ever* seen him doubt himself in any context. He never voiced that he felt baseball was expected of him and I never voiced that it was. Still, both he and his little brother must have supposed that their baseball-happy dad would be pleased if they excelled at the game, even if I didn't demand that of them.

We enjoyed the movie and the baseball season that followed close on its heels. The following year Max did go to tryouts and, despite that he wasn't drafted into the majors, had the finest season of his brief career in youth baseball. What he accomplished that summer somehow spilled over into the rest of his life. Or maybe it was the other way around.

As for, *Miracle,* there's quite a back story there...

That film is the stirring account of the 1980 Olympic hockey game between the United States and the Soviet Union.

We saw it on February 7, 2004; Chris, Ben, myself and a limo full of Ben's pals partying in celebration of Ben's 10th birthday the day before.

Limo? Yes, and here's why: one holiday season the staff at the pub had surprised our family by sending a limousine to our house to take us all on a tour of local holiday light displays. Ben in particular was impressed. Then in December of 2003 I arranged an extended family stag trip to Kansa City to see the Bears play the Chiefs on my brother Mark's birthday. The problem there was that none of us had a vehicle big enough for all of us, so I hired the same limo service from the holiday lights tour to drive us there and back. Well, the heater didn't work right, the music system didn't work right, the Bears got beat, our seats were practically in the last row, etc. The only bright spot of the day was the unseasonably warm, sunny weather.

Our driver was embarrassed by the various malfunctions of his vehicle so when he dropped us off at day's end he told me that I was entitled to a free service at my convenience as a gesture of compensation. So, a couple months later, we took him up on it as part of Ben's birthday gala. We even took a picture of all the boys posed by the stretch with Steve, the chaffeur.

The movie was great!

I forget how many months later we saw the article in the paper about Steve going to prison for driving adolescent boys around and tickling them in his limo.

Just another argument in favor of mass transit.

The Fielder's Choice

Just after school recessed for the summer of 2008 Ben's Senior League team - agonizingly named the Cardinals - was playing one of its last games of that season on a Saturday afternoon at the Raccoon Valley complex.

Ben was on 1st base after a base hit when the batter who followed him tapped a roller bashfully up the 3rd base line. The ball came to a stop in the grass at about the same instant that the charging 3rd baseman plucked it up. His momentum was more toward 1st base than 2nd. Plus, there was Ben's decent speed on the base paths to consider. The throw should logically have been intended to apprehend the batter. Instead it was aimed towards the middle of the diamond in an attempt to force out the runner headed there.

The ball and Ben arrived simultaneously at 2nd base. As he stretched into his slide his head aligned perfectly with the throw's line of flight. It came in just beneath the brim of the helmet that protected most of Ben's head besides his face. Ben's toe hit the bag and the ball hit his eye, the left one, flush and undeflected.

He was safe. He was hurt.

Ben's hands covered his face. He got to his feet right away and started jogging towards the dugout. I was waiting for him there and was stunned to see that in just those few seconds his eye had already swollen nearly shut. It was like the bumps on the head sustained by Looney Tunes characters that rise immediately to freakish dimensions.

Somebody ran to the concession stand to get ice. Somebody else ran around the grounds in search of a doctor. We laid Ben down on his back and I think he started to get frightened by what he was seeing in other people's faces when they looked at his.

Some sort of a doctor arrived and, in a spirit of erring on the cautious side, he put out a call for an ambulance. At that point I became really glad that I was the only one in Ben's cheering section that day.

I don't remember where his siblings were but his mother and grandmother were at a wedding shower. That was mostly to the good, but it meant that I now had to call and casually report that the game was going well and, oh yeah, Ben got hit in the eye and would be riding to the ER in an ambulance and I'll meet you there and so how's the shower anyway? Good cake?

I rode shotgun in the ambulance and tried to make nice with the crew in hopes that Ben would be reassured if he saw that I was not alarmed. Meanwhile visions of Tony Conigliaro were racing in my head.

Tony C. was a young slugger for the Boston Red Sox in the late 1960's whose career took off like a rocket before it was snuffed out when he was hit in the eye by a pitch. I couldn't get the image of a famous picture of his swollen, discolored eye out of my mind.

Ben never lost consciousness. His orbital bone was fractured beneath the eye when it did its anatomical job and absorbed most of the shock of the ball's impact. Over the course of the next several weeks of that summer his vision fully restored. Of course his baseball seasons ended on that play, both the one at Raccoon Valley that had nearly run its course and the one as a member of the Roosevelt freshman team that had barely begun.

For a time his injury was offset by the attention he basked in. There were lots of phone calls of concern. Team cards were delivered by delegations of players and coaches. He even drew a certain pride from a particularly distorted mug shot type photo that was taken not long after he sustained the injury; once his boyish good looks started to return and he knew he wouldn't always look like he'd gone 15 rounds with the champ, that is.

But even though Ben dodged, if not the ball itself, the most serious consequences it might have inflicted, his summer was pretty well shot.

The doctor's orders even precluded swimming for most of the pool season. Worst of all, medically speaking, was the session with a surgeon we'd been referred to by an ophthalmologist. After nagging Ben pretty much all his life to blow his nose rather than snort its contents back up towards his centers of higher learning, I had to sit and listen to a board certified neurosurgeon explain in my son's presence why, actually, blowing was not good for the sinus cavity, with or without a facial fracture.

That was the first time I remember Ben grinning that summer.

He could even have winked at me left-eyed if he'd wanted to.

Time Out

Of course we have taken our share of pictures over the years. In fact, we've accumulated boxes full of them. They are scattered about the house randomly like so many spare buttons, rubber bands and paper clips. I suppose the day may come when, freed from more pressing day to day responsibilities, Chris and I will pass time together cataloging them into some semblance of order, reconstructing the bewildering chronology of our coparentship.

Without doing that there is one in particular that has always struck me. It is the exception that proves my rule; a veritable needle of poignancy in a haystack of ho-hum. It depicts one of our children at about the age of three. He is aloft, just beyond the reach of my outstretched arms. The child is aglow and obviously laughing, airborne because of having been tossed up like a bale of boy.

But the effect of the photo on me has always been that he appears to be dropping from the sky towards a waiting embrace. If it were captioned the caption would read: Heaven Sent.

Once More With Feelings

As Max's senior and Ben's freshman year of high school got underway the three of us made the next in our series of junkets to Chicago to see what the Cubs were up to over the Labor Day weekend in 2008.

For Ben it was sort of a rally in the bottom of that summer's 9th inning.

The Phillies were in town and we had tickets to two games. For one of them I bought cheap seats in the upper deck grandstand. For the other we had field boxes on the aisle, behind the plate, courtesy of my old umpire friend, Eric.

His crew wasn't working the series, but I'd e-mailed him earlier in the summer to see if he could help us out. By then I really couldn't afford what had become almost routine trips to Wrigley Field over the years, so I swallowed some pride and reached out to Eric for the first time since I'd sworn off doing that on the grounds that it disentitled me to my occasional upset with modern umpiring.

But now I sensed that it might be quite a while before me and my sons would do this again, so I asked, and Eric obliged again.

The Cubs were having quite a season in 2008. They'd been cruising along with the best record in the National League all summer. It was the centennial anniversary of their last world championship season. The silly symmetry of that appealed to my OCD side and, combined with their gaudy winning percentage, lent credence to the hope/suspicion that *this* finally, really, incredibly, belatedly was the year!

The Cubs lost the upper deck game without mustering so much as an extra base hit.

We endured it from our remote perch just in front of some young folks intent on breaking the park record for mai tais in a nine inning game. They were mostly oblivious to us but the group in front of us made the mistake of turning and scowling at one of their profane, if cheerful, outbursts during the game. That of course went neither unnoticed nor unchallenged. They became even more boisterous now that they had a closer ranged target than the players down there somewhere on the field far below.

Alas, we were in a lawless section where ushers did not preside. As a matter of fact we were in the same general area where I'd gone down a long time ago while stumbling up the steep, concrete steps with a tray of beers. On that occasion I was approximately the same age as our neighbors to the rear were on this one. My drunken fall resulted in a nasty incision in my forehead that required my removal from the ballpark on a gurney for transport to a local ER and stitching. It was messy but I was feeling no pain. In fact, I saw no need for stitches at the hospital and made it as difficult as possible for them to be installed.

Someone had to be called in to talk to me and calm me down. When I came to from that episode there was a card in my wallet with the fellow's name and number on it and a suggestion that I call him if ever I wanted help with my drinking problem. I never used it but have marked that incident ever since as the first time that anyone ever suggested, at least to me, that I might be an alcoholic.

Out of the mouths of strangers...

I couldn't tell you exactly what year that happened. I wasn't yet in the habit of hanging on to much of anything, let alone ticket stubs.

The boys actually got a certain kick out of the language and antics they were exposed to that afternoon, certainly more of one than the lackluster ballgame offered. And for my part, I was just glad that it wasn't their father causing the ruckus.

The next day we picked up our big shot tickets at the will-call window - they had $0.00 printed on them where $75.00 should have been - and were issued that day's promotional gimmick when we presented them at the turnstiles. Everyone was given a scratch off ticket offering the chance to win one of a hundred official major league balls autographed by Alfonso Soriano, the Cubs' most overpaid alleged superstar. In a crowd of roughly 40,000 each of us was about a 400 to 1 shot. I scratched; sorry. Ben scratched; sorry. Max scratched – *YOU'RE A WINNER!*

It wasn't exactly a lottery jackpot, but at the time it made all three of us feel chosen, especially when we arrived at our high definition seats.

Ben was wearing a "Fukudome is my homey" [that rhymes, incidentally, for those not hip to the phonetics of the Cub roster] t-shirt fresh off the sidewalk rack outside the ballpark. They were all the rage that summer before it became clear that Kosuke Fukudome, the Cubs' right fielder, was a multimillion dollar flash from Japan. He'd socked a dramatic game-tying three-run homer in the bottom of the 9th on Opening Day in April and gotten off to a fast start, but was melting like the wicked witch of the far east in the dog days of late summer.

Max had shopped the street vendors for a souvenir to deliver back home to his girlfriend as part of his campaign to indoctrinate her into the Cub cult. She had a father with some emotional ties to the White Sox, but nothing on the level of our disorder. She would be easily swayed by the feminine styled t-shirt he picked out for her, as long as she weren't offended by the size he guessed at.

In that department he asked my advice. This was an aspect not part of our previous expeditions to this part of the world. But there was some precedent for Max enlisting my help in affairs of the heart.

When he was about to enter 6th grade he confided in me that he intended to ask a ballerina he knew from church if she might like to affiliate with him. It was a matter complicated by logistics. They attended different schools, the adolescent equivalent of a bi-coastal romance. But he had reason to expect a favorable answer based on the way the girl had thrown herself at him on a church outing to an Iowa Cubs game that summer.

He sought some guidance as to how to present his offer. I asked him what he saw in this girl that had him in such a dither.

"Well," he said, "she's smart and she's real popular, and she must like baseball…" then he paused for effect before adding, "and let's face it – she *is* a knockout."

She turned him down in favor of a better offer from a kid who was a Yankee fan, a pal of Max's from elementary school with whom he reunited as a high school freshman. By then the girl who came between them was out of the way of a friendship that would later survive Greg's family moving to Vermont.

A lot had changed since we three first came together to Wrigley Field. But not everything. The Cubs dropped another one that day, again without so much as an extra base hit. The pitcher for the Phillies was Jamie Moyer, a decrepit old southpaw who was older than my wife and threw about as hard as she does. He was much too old to be named Jamie. Usually live attendance at a big league game produces awe for the players' talents that mere TV cannot. Particularly impressive is the velocity of the pitches. Not in Moyer's case. From where we were sitting it looked like I could dig in against him and make some contact.

We'd billed our trip as a possible playoff preview since the Phillies had a good young team, the grizzled Moyer notwithstanding, but we didn't realize how good. It turned out that they were peaking for a run that would culminate with a World Series championship in the fall.

But in the moment we couldn't get past the fact that the Cubs' offensive output for the weekend consisted of 22 mere singles which bounced off of the Philadelphians like salt shaken at a charging steer.

That night we had better luck at a good steakhouse near The Magnificent Mile. We sat at a sidewalk table and, as usual, Ben and I had glorified cheeseburgers and Max had a filet so big he couldn't finish it. On our walk back to the hotel after dinner he gave what remained of it to a homeless fella sitting against a building on a bustling street corner in the loop. The stranger too had steak on the sidewalk that evening.

The next day, Labor Day, we drove home with the car radio tuned to the Cub game. The Astros had replaced the Phillies as our tormentors and would shut us out that day, the 3rd in a rubber band of losses that began the day we arrived in town and would stretch later in the week all the way to six before it snapped. Again that day no Cub ran further than 1st base out of the batter's box.

By the time I switched off the radio in frustration somewhere on the home side of the Mississippi the brothers had already retreated into their respective iPods. They were my passengers, but I wondered in a moment of self-sorrow what else were they now? Their courses were not so much mine to steer any more. I too was being switched off.

The Midnight Ride

The fall of 2008 was rather frenetic for me, especially considering that I was not employed. Simultaneously, I, a strict mono-tasker, was in the process of publishing my first book, coordinating a college search and gearing up for the Cubs' post-season push toward the World Series. So it wasn't just that three balls were in the air so much as it was that each of them represented something important.

In early October the Cubs lightened the load when they were summarily whisked from the playoffs in the minimum of three games at the hands of the Los Angeles Dodgers, a demise so stunningly unceremonious that I contrived an observance to mark it.

On the morning after the final defeat I took a small garbage pail from the garage, placed it in the middle of the driveway, threw my Cub hat in, squirted it with a brief spray of lighter fluid and tossed in a lit match while mumbling a liturgy of profanities appropriate to the occasion. Then I moved on to more important business.

During Max's junior year he and I had taken a whirlwind tour of some prospective schools in the Midwest. St. Olaf wasn't on his list. We checked out Lawrence University in Appleton, Wisconsin and then swung down through Chicago to see Northwestern, DePaul and Columbia College. At that point DePaul emerged as his early frontrunner based on its music school. Coincidentally, enrollment there would have placed him in Lincoln Park, just two "L" stops from Wrigley Field.

Also on his preliminary list were an assortment of conservatories in the east, but now, as the process intensified for seniors, the list was pared by other factors.

The girl Max had started dating that summer was a freshman at Butler in Indianapolis. He was adamant about *not* going there, but was now more inclined to limit his radius to 500 miles or so from Des Moines. Chicago and Indianapolis are only about 150 miles apart so going to school there would at least enable reciprocal campus visits if the relationship endured.

Max 's focus was on DePaul but his parents pointed out that, if only as a formality, he needed to apply to some other schools too. We suggested Drake as a local alternative in hopes that a desire to keep homegrown talent around might lead to more lucrative scholarship offers. And Butler too was floated as a possibility. Abby's attendance there had led to some research which revealed that the school's Jordan College of Fine Arts had a long and distinguished pedigree. That coupled with additional liberal arts education besides musical training and the school's small size within a larger urban setting made Butler a legitimate contender on the basis of other criteria that were more objective than Abby's presence on campus. We convinced him that it made sense to at least apply there. Grudgingly, he agreed.

Before and after playing the title role in his high school's fall production of *Jesus Christ Superstar* Max was also in effect getting his own small business up and running as the front man for assorted jazz combos playing gigs around the Des Moines area. He'd had traditional high school part-time jobs ever since he was 15 as a grocery sacker, an onion ringer at a greasy spoon, a library page and a restaurant host. But now he was making good and regular money playing with older professional musicians at both public venues and private events.

By the time my book was launched in mid-December at a local independent bookstore Max was almost as much role model to me as son. He had an absolute belief in himself that I both admired and envied. I wondered how I could have been involved in something that was so foreign to me.

The night of the book release, which fell precisely on Emma's 12th birthday, December 19th, bordered on overwhelming for the author. There wasn't much advance notice, owing to my inexperience and disorganization. Plus the weather was poor and it was an otherwise especially busy time of the year. Yet people came and lined up to buy my book and have it signed. It was heady stuff for an out-of-work bartender. I hadn't been so sweaty and knock-kneed since our wedding day.

The most memorable part of the experience for me came while I was reading a passage from the book about my own father. My mouth felt as dry as my brow felt damp. I could feel Ben seated behind me, listening more attentively than I thought he ever had to anything I'd had to say directly to him. And out of the corner of one eye I could see Max off to the side in front of me. The look on his face was one I'd never seen there before and yet it was familiar. He looked the way I remember feeling upon the births of he and his brother and sister. I shall remember that look just as vividly.

A month later, after the holiday dust had settled, Max and I took off on his college audition tour. Besides that you have to go to them instead of them scouting you as they do athletes, it is another curse of the prospective fine arts major that your college admissions decisions are delayed beyond the audition months of January and February.

The first stop for Max turned out to be Butler early on a Friday morning in late January. Since he had a regular Thursday night gig at a supper club in Des Moines we faced an all-night drive to Indianapolis with me at the wheel while he tried to grab some shut-eye in the shotgun seat.

It was quite a ride.

We'd not traveled under the guidance of a GPS device before. Somebody gave one to Max at Christmas as a practical symbol of the threshold he stood upon. He was on the verge of some real exploration in his life and, besides that, he wasn't exactly from a long line of pathfinders.

When we were programming our destination we first selected a slightly accented, sultry voice from the gizmo's stable that we would have ridden anywhere. By the time we left Chris had swapped it out for a sterner, more matronly tone.

Not only were we traveling way beyond my customary curfew, it was also very dark outside. I was tired, peripherally blind and anxious. Luckily the weather was about as good as it gets during January in the Midwest. Had a winter storm descended upon our route we'd surely have perished. As it was we made our way with me gripping the wheel as though clinging to the edge of a precipice, letting go occasionally with one hand to grab and gulp some sort of caffeinated beverage.

Somewhere in the void between Peoria and our destination Max was awakened by the urge to pee, a syndrome I'd become familiar with since passing the half century marker.

It was the middle of night in the middle of winter in the middle of nowhere. A couple of interstate exits came and went that didn't offer the lit-up, all-night, truck stop ambience I was looking for; a place where I could refuel and recaffeinate while Max did what it was time for him to do.

When he could no longer contain himself I veered down a ramp that boasted of a convenience store in the nearest whistle-stop village, the sort of joint that tends to be open 24/7 in metropolitan areas.

While the GPS repeatedly advised us to turn around we forged ahead into the black unknown like a pair of disobedient whipping boys ignoring their dominatrix.

Finally, several miles off course, we came to the phonetically correct "Kum & Go," which I remember thinking at the time would make a good name for the inevitable chain of brothels that will someday spread across the land. It was closed. Max left his mark on the grounds while I waited in the car and absorbed a verbal spanking from our navigator that kept me awake.

Back on the road Max slept, or tried to, in an uncomfortable seat while I sang, not lullabyes, but howls designed to keep the driver awake.

A few hours later we arrived in Indianapolis about the same time as an unusually welcome and pretty sunrise that was very truly a sight for my sore eyes.

We made our way to Butler's campus while Max roused himself. We stopped at Abby's dorm so he could say hello before she headed off to classes. Then he slipped into the lobby restroom, splashed some water on his face and changed into his work clothes as though he were slipping into a phone booth and donning a cape.

We traded places. I napped and he sang.

Going Solo

Having given Max a laptop a year prior when we moved as an early graduation gift, we groped now for something to mark the actual occasion as it drew near.

I ordered four Cub tickets for May 27, 2009, three days after commencement. They weren't in the family section this time. We gave them to Max and told him to invite three buddies. When the day arrived we watched him climb on his bike, er, into the car, and ride away.

He called that afternoon from the bleachers at Wrigley Field. I'd been listening to the game on the radio at home. When the phone rang I knew it was him. Our old pal Carlos Zambrano had just been tossed from the game after one of his better tantrums. Then he really got mad, gesturing as though he were ejecting the umpire who'd ejected him and trying to throw the ball from just in front of the plate to the leftfield bleachers where Max and his friends were seated. It was just like old times - almost.

The wireless network that linked our telephones that day wasn't the only connection that spanned the physical distance between us.

After we hung up I must have felt a little sorry for myself. This was another benchmark along the timeline that included the first day of school, the first choral solo, the maiden voyage as a licensed driver and, I was left to suspect, some other firsts that had not come to my direct attention and probably were not my business.

Our days of living together were dwindling fast now and it was easy to lapse into episodes of flashback. It was commonplace by then for me to compare and contrast Max's life with what I remembered about my own at various stages since he, as the lead dog in our litter, was the first to arrive at various places in life where I'd already been. But more and more now this was becoming an exercise in realization that he was exploring where I'd not gone. His high school years were put to much better use than my own even though they were passed at the same physical place as mine.

I can tell you that my parents would have been guilty of gross negligence had they sent me off to Chicago with friends mere days after my high school graduation. Years later when I first started making such trips as a nominal adult they often fell into the category of hair-raising, even life-threatening.

That was not the case with our 17 year-old son. It was nice to hear from him that day, calling from a place I *was* familiar with, a place that I first took him to and was glad that he was fond of with or without my company.

I hung up the phone like a relay runner pulls up and pulls over after passing the baton.

Role Reversal

On Thursday, July 23, 2009, about a month before he was to leave home for college and, in a sense, for good, Max and I went out to dinner at the downtown restaurant where he was working part-time; just the two of us. For dessert we walked over to that evening's Iowa Cubs game.

The outing started with the feel of a kept tradition about it. It might have been an occasion for deep reflection, the offering of advice and wisdom, that sort of thing. But I don't recall anything

in particular that we talked about. We were too busy shelling peanuts and doing something together for the first time that summer
that we used to do together a lot. There was also the feel of last
time for a long time in the air.

Where was the kindergartner who'd flown with me to Chicago
for Opening Day? What happened to the birthday boy from the
All-Star game in Seattle? Now my companion was a good-look-
ing, good-natured young man full of confidence and plans and
his own opinions about everything from the designated hitter to
global warming.

During the game there was a marriage proposal beamed up on the
scoreboard's video screen. An obviously pregnant young woman
threw her arms around the young man who'd just become her fi-
ance as the PA announcer exulted, "it looks like she said, 'YES'!"

I mentioned that she'd apparently said yes to this fella some time
ago in more private circumstances, which caused some giggling
in front of us and brought a slightly embarrassed grin to Max's
face. I was reminded of how I used to be able to sense him and
Ben watching and listening when I'd holler at ballgames, looking
for clues and cues as to the protocol and jargon of the ballpark.
Before he found his own voice Max served an apprenticeship as
an enthused, engaged mimicker of his sometimes loudmouthed
father.

We left after the 7th inning stretch by mutual agreement, a reflection of the general irrelevance of final scores in the minor leagues.
I could have stayed there all night but I knew he had other places
to go and other people to see. I was touched that it was he who'd

made a point of this and that he had done so only partly because he thought *I* would enjoy it.

And so I did, but in ways very different from the usual ones. For the first time I had the sensation of being taken to a ballgame by him instead of the other way around. He even dropped me at home before he drove off and resumed the normal speed of his life, one I could no longer keep up with.

Off to College

In late August we packed the largest of our three small cars with Max and the tip of his personal effects and headed for Indianapolis to deliver him to college. There wasn't room for Ben and Emma. The night before he left Max treated them to a night at the Iowa state fair.

I was a week into a new job with the Des Moines school district.

The trip was like giving him life a second time. For 18 years we'd been giving him a good share of ours. Now we were handing him his own.

We spent the night we arrived in a downtown hotel and shared a pizza. The next morning we emptied the car into his dorm room and then drove to the nearest Target and refilled it with laundry detergent and other stuff we'd never bought for him before.

That night Chris and I lay awake in the same hotel room Max had shared with us the night before. There seemed to be a draft blowing through the gaping hole where he had been. When the darkness passed finally into the light of the next day we rose, had breakfast and drove back to campus to look at him and touch him again. Then we drove home. It was a full day's work. We passed the miles swapping anecdotes: his first solo session on the throne, the proceeds of which were bagged and frozen until I got home from work so I could behold the creation and praise the creator; the time Chris rushed him off to a middle school flag football game in too-tight sweat pants and then had to listen to girls giggling at him in the stands; the time he dove right into the lake on our summer vacation, swam up to a group of girls, surfaced and announced, Hi! My name's Max. I'm from Des Moines;" the time on another vacation when he hooked a nice walleye just as the clock was running out on the kids' fishing contest at the lodge where we were staying and thrust the pole into Ben's hands so his little brother won first prize; the times when we stood with an auditorium full of people and applauded the performances as Jean Valjean and Jesus Christ of a flat-footed, clumsy kid who got assigned to a baseball fan father and tried to beat his ball playing school chums at their own game rather than play to his own natural strengths.

When we got home Ben and Emma and Mitt and Maple were waiting.

We rearranged.

The Show Goes On

About a month after Max had left the fold life thrust a flash-back in my path.

My job with the school district involved me with an event designed to get kids who'd dropped out of school to rethink and come back. Targets were identified and located and teams were dispatched to knock on their doors and extend the invitations.

My squad met at Roosevelt on the appointed Saturday morning and was given our roster of dropouts. I scanned it and one ex-student's name stood out. At first I wasn't sure why. But as we made our rounds it finally came to me. By the time we parked in the driveway of the kid whose name had rung a distant bell earlier that morning, I'd fixed on who he was.

And so there I was knocking on the door of *The Crapper*. Almost five years after the 8th grade Halloween party I'd finally caught up with him. Except that he wasn't home. It was, after all, early on a Saturday morning and he hadn't yet come home from Friday night.

His home looked nice. His mother was nice. She spoke in terms and tones that sounded like she was more hopeful the program would reach kids other than her own. Maybe she knew him too well. Maybe she knew him as well as I knew Max who was 500 miles away that morning fighting off his first bout of homesickness with a strong dose of practice, practice, practice.

The Crapper was somewhere nearby not wanting to come home. What made the difference between these kids? What made one a valedictorian and the other a dropout? I'm not sure Max liked high school any more than his counterpart; he just made the most of it instead of the least. It didn't look like he'd come from any nicer home or that his parents were any better.

The certainty that we *were* luckier constipated any retaliatory thoughts of taking, or rather leaving, my revenge as I walked back down the driveway.

We left a phone number that no one there has ever called.

In Lieu of Pictures

There are baseballs scattered throughout our house like lymph nodes.

Besides the ones in my underwear drawer are another dozen scattered across a shelf behind my desk in what passes for a home office. In the basement, stored out of sight and mind in a translucent plastic box are 10 or so more. I run across those every year when it's time to rummage around and relocate the Christmas trimmings. Ben has some randomly arrayed in his bedroom. So does Max. I think Emma even has one rather garish pink one imprinted with a Cub logo that stands out as both the most expensive and least authentic one in our haphazard, uncatalogued collection. It was a token I bought on a trip she wasn't part of to reassure her that she was in my thoughts while not in my company.

The others range from old little league relics to ones tossed or swatted into our possession by real live big leaguers.

There are some that bear autographs of ballplayers who seemed important enough at times that I thought those should be taken out of service, as it were, and preserved in a pristine condition inside protective plastic cubes. Lacking my sense of sentimentality, Ben was not above putting some of them into play occasionally out in the yard when no other balls were handy. The scuff marks and smudges have become as much the story in those cases as the original acquisition of the souvenir.

Were I gigantic I could imagine myself filling a bowl with the balls, pouring on memories like milk, sprinkling them with spoonfuls of sugary embellishment and taking nourishment from them as from a bowl of cereal.

If I ever fancied myself a collector of memorabilia I became somewhere along the way one of a different stripe than I must have started out to be.

Besides the balls, I maintain a small, private cache of baseball cards that are of more value to me than anyone else would ever ascribe to them.

I have a Rocky Colavito card just because his is maybe my favorite ballplayer name of all-time. I also admired the way he used to used to loosen up in the on-deck circle before stepping to the plate, holding his bat at both ends behind his back and raising it up toward his shoulders. That always hurt when I tried to imitate it. Colavito must have been hinged with double jointed shoulders.

There's an Eddie Murray card I acquired after he was elected to the Hall of Fame and I discovered he and I share the same birthday.

Naturally there are assorted cards of former Cubs - Ernie Banks, Billy Williams, Ron Santo, Ryne Sandberg, Fergie Jenkins - most of which were awarded as game day promtions at Wrigley Field and some of which have been signed.

I have a Mickey Mantle card that's important to me on the ironic grounds that I remember wanting to be like him when I grew up and eventually discovered that I was in the sense that we were both alcoholics.

Mixed in with all the others is my Ben Wellman card. It was taken on photo day when he was 10, a 4'6" rookie with the Raccoon Valley Cubs. He's posed in his left-handed batting stance, looking menacingly towards an out of frame, imaginary, overmatched pitcher. He autographed it for me, using a blue marker that was not very finely pointed and better suited for postering.

Whatever I felt about sports in general and baseball in particular before I became a father doesn't matter anymore. They have changed and so have I. When the kids were growing up I shared ballgames with them because they were one of the relatively few things I thought I knew anything about. Not anything important; anything at all. I gave them what I could of what I had. I enjoyed their company and I wanted them to enjoy mine.

Perhaps ballgames were over-emphasized at the expense of other nuances of life. I'm thinking at the moment of cribbage and driving a manual transmission, two vanishing arts that I am trained in and should pass on before it's too late.

Peer Pressure

Parenting is fraught with pitfalls. But they don't all have to do with kids. The sorest spot for me has been the extent to which having children forces you to rub elbows with other parents. At its best this can afford some chance for commiseration, brain picking and note comparison. There has been some of each of those. But more often I've had the sense of wandering naively into a no holds barred game of one-upsmanship.

The realization dawned gradually and harmlessly at first.

Before the kids were in school we'd run into people out and about. If your toddler sniffles they launch into a medical lecture complete with reviews of all the pediatricians in town. If you relate some cute, charming anecdote you're admonished to cherish the memory because the boom is soon to be lowered. If you innocently mention that you haven't really given much thought to colleges yet [preoccupied with toilet training] brace for the rundown on the twin kindergartners, Awesome and Winsome, and their off the charts performance on the Parents Undermining Kids' Education [PUKE] matrix, a subjective predictor of Ivy League prospects for the newly walking.

But the pre-school years are a wading pool compared to the maelstrom that ensues at the schoolhouse door.

I was astonished by the brazenness of the modern parent's vanities.

When Max was in kindergarten we went to Open House at his school, the same one where I'd started out nearly forty years earlier.

I was spotted in the crowded central hallway by a fellow father, a jackass from way back who was a couple years behind me in school.

"What are *YOU* doing here?" he demanded, as though greeting Beelzebub at church on Easter Sunday.

Full disclosure would include that our paths had not crossed since I'd abandoned a self-destructive lifestyle that dated to our own schooldays. He may have just been surprised to see me still alive. He surely knew that a libertine such as he perceived me to be was properly equipped and trained for reproduction. But his tone suggested disbelief that I hadn't been sterilized by court order.

I was speechless.

A few years later the rotten luck of the draw resulted in the same fellow's assignment as Ben's basketball coach in a pee-wee league.

I came around the corner of the cereal aisle one day in mid-season and there he was; our carts practically collided, so I had no chance to elude him with my grocery store getaway maneuvers.

"I'm concerned about Ben," he told me, the way a tough cop might talk to a suspect's dad. "It's his ball-handling." The only thing I'd really noticed about the team was that Son of Jackass shot the ball every time he touched it.

"I've got some concerns about Ben too," I said, "but ball-handling isn't even on the list."

We were knocked a bit off our stride in the early school years. Dismayed by the naked competitiveness around us at a time when we were becoming more involved at our church and I was relatively new in sobriety we followed a neighboring family to a new private, Christian school; the academy mentioned earlier. Not long after moving the boys there Max came home talking about an altar call that day during an assembly. This news was like a rubber hammer tapping just below our Episcopalian knee-caps. We couldn't believe that parents weren't consulted before their children were invited to accept Christ as their personal savior in between lunch and recess. By our repressed standards this equated to asking for volunteers during sex education. We met with the principal and explained that both Max and Ben had been baptized at our church shortly after they were born. He in turn explained that the school deemed "infant sprinklings" as insufficient and invalid spiritual inoculation. Having flunked the litmus test we beat a quick retreat back to public school.

When Emma was in 5th grade and just approaching the outskirts of the middle school social jungle, Chris encountered another 5th grade mother at a PTA meeting. This woman's cause célèbre was the "Gifted and Talented" [aka, her kids] agenda [let's make sure the budget includes plenty of stationery and bumper stickers].

While working as a low-level functionary for our local school district I put together a database on school board actions by prowling through minutes of old meetings. There, I even found a reference to this woman as a parent of "highly gifted children" when she appeared as the mother of grammar schoolers to lobby on behalf of some cutting edge high school curricula that her baby-toothed savants will probably skip over when their times come anyway. So it's on the record; her stuff is top-grade.

The two moms got to chatting about how their girls were faring outside of the classroom. Emma had been confiding some confusion as to why everybody didn't seem to operate by the same rules we'd imposed upon her. Chris shared that Emma was having some difficulties just then on the social front.

"Really?" said her counterpart. "Lilac [a loose translation of her Native American name, Fawn With Odorless Droppings] is quite popular."

Max's grade school watershed happened in the "Battle of the Books," a competitive contrivance for the benefit of the nimbler readers' parents. He missed a question that eliminated his school's team from the tournament at the local level and shrugged it off. But one of his teammates, the son of their parent "coach," burst into tears and was badly scarred by the time he'd stopped, dropped & rolled.

The euphemism currently in vogue for the Triple A [athletics, academics and arts] conceit of moms and dads is "advocate for my child" as in the response, "I was just trying to be an advocate for my child," to the prosecutor's question: "Mrs. Vicarious, why did you hire the Tonya Harding gang to escort the kid home from school who beat out your daughter for 1st chair tambourine?"

It is the curse of the camcorder and it is powerful.

If you start 'em out with commencement exercises at pre-school, the law of escalation ensures that high school spring breaks and bachelor/bachelorette parties will become transcontinental operations.

You should see the extravaganza that's now held annually on graduation night at the high school I thought I'd left behind in 1972. One of these years I expect they'll be taking bids for the television rights. It's supposed to be in the spirit of keeping the newly minted graduates from having their celebration marred by tragedy, but if that was the event's origin it takes a backseat now to bare-knuckled parents engaged in an event-planning variation of "can you top this." One year's class sets the bar for the next much like annual fundraising campaigns seek to nudge ever upward.

What's hardest to understand is not that we marvel at our offspring. We ought to. It's how anxious we've become to give them to the world. It is inevitable that this be done, but in the meantime and while we can, why not hoard them? It is a hard thing to settle for them being the most interesting people we know and not insist on telling other people why. I guess you are reading a case in point.

Teaching them to ride a bike is the whole thing in a nutshell. You, the steadying influence running alongside until suddenly they're doing it without your help and away they go leaving in their wake a melancholy amazement and the flickering but inextinguishable memory of the moment you met.

Furthermore

B esides the frontal assaults of rival parents, your emotional flanks are permanently exposed. You write a blank check, reasonably sure that there will be a steady supply of joys and celebrations and milestones and highpoints. You do not pause long to weigh the potentials for heartbreak, tragedy, disappointment and raw deals.

Like a mountain climber, for a parent to look ahead is also to look up. And you know the amazing thing? For all the people who arrive finally at epilogues that are difficult for parent and child alike; for all those who are lost on the descent from the summits; for all the Alzheimer sentences and estranged loved ones and unresolved resentments and stuffed grief and petty jealousies, there isn't much warning and advice passed back down the mountain to turn back. Yes, there are plenty whose climbs end in divorce. They find themselves not up to it but wish they were and many try again.

Given the large number of folks with gripes about their family of origin there are remarkably few who don't start over and make a new one for themselves.

It is an exhilarating mess and an all-consuming treasure hunt. It is an expedition in search of nothing less than immortality, even for those who scoff at eternal life as the folly of the pious. It's sometimes hard to appreciate when your perspective is the up close one of used diapers or endless soccer schedules or driver training or preposterous haircuts or clothes that are expensive because they look cheap and worn out or grunted, mumbled responses to earnest attempts at engagement or, worst of all, the realization that you have become, for the time being at least, an embarrassment; your children's secret love.

You are tethered in the storms on the icy, slippery slopes to one or more who wonder how they could possibly have come from you. You chose to make the climb with them without knowing who they were, but they had no choice in the matter at all. And the appealing risk of it all is that if one of you falls so do the others, offset by the maxim that footing is better together than on one's own. The price for the journey is incalculable from a minimum of more than you can spare to a max out of more than you can bear. And still people line up to sign up.

Making Rounds

There is a lot to miss as kids grow up and leave stage after stage of their rocketing lives behind. Photos and videos do preserve a certain residue I suppose. But it's not the ballgames and the school programs or the church Christmas pageants – most definitely not the school programs or the church Christmas pageants – that are to be missed when they're gone. How could it be the external events staged away from home? Sometimes the ways we document the special events and occasions don't do them justice anyway. Instead of engaging that Pavlovian emotional drool we count on them for, they reveal that it was nothing more than yet another school program or church Christmas pageant. You run the risk of feeling disentitled to your sentimentality.

We at our house are not boastless. But our kids have also had their shares of zits and poor grades and been uninvited and laughed at. If there is a Recommended Daily Allowance of adoration there is likely also a limit beyond which the stuff does more harm than good. Unless it's given to them like money stashed in an account they don't know of, say during the bedtime rounds when all of them were small and ran out of gas before I did at the end of each day.

Stealing into their bedrooms and looking down at them sleeping was like going through an art gallery. I could just stand there and contemplate.

Sunrises and sunsets get a lot of recognition as awe-inspiring yet routine events. Part of the typical description of the feelings they engender is that they make the observer feel small. I'm all for humility and I'm not debunking the majesty of the daily solar ups and downs. But I'm here to make a case for the bedtime rounds on the grounds that they make a father feel very big.

And Now?

One weekend this month Max drove the thousand or so mile round trip between his current outpost and headquarters to keep an open-ended promise he'd made some time ago to sing at a particular funeral when it came. He sang two songs. The next weekend he made the same trip to sing two more songs, this time at the big-bucks-per-plate annual gala of a local community arts group in hopes of lining up support for a big concert he's planning for next summer. In between and after the road trips he continued the life of a college freshman.

We weather his journeys surprisingly well considering that we were white-knuckling him backing out of the driveway just a couple of years ago. Now we're at that stage with Ben who just got his driver's license.

Max's visits home usually are followed by his father going to the bank to deposit money the kid earned performing around town. The last couple of times I've done that have been two-birds-with-one-stone errands that made for interesting comparison. In both cases I also had checks in my pocket that I'd earned writing.

The first time Max's gig loot roughly matched my royalty check. It was a crude and misleading equivalence, especially when you factor in the cash tips he took back to school with him and note that I was banking the proceeds from a calendar quarter's worth of sales of a book that was a year-plus in the making and he was stashing wages earned in several hours of performing.

On the next round his deposit was substantial enough to split between his checking and savings accounts; my meager freelance check was converted into a few days' worth of walking around money.

Besides suggesting that Max has a higher ceiling as a musician than I do as a writer that vignette also hints again at the good example he's been for his father. I thought I was supposed to show him how to go for it. It has been more the other way around.

He has acknowledged that there was a time in his life when he worried that he wasn't cut out to be what he figured his dad had hoped for in a son. When he was grappling with those sorts of issues I sensed as much and wanted to address them and be reassuring. Instead I was clumsy in walking the fine line between letting him know that it was okay if he didn't play in the big leagues and telling him that he didn't stand a chance [in a spirit of releasing him from some perceived obligation] before he figured that out for himself.

He became enough of a ballplayer to prove something to both of us before he stopped playing on his own terms; on the grounds that his clearest talents would be better served in other milieus.

The chats we had on the mound when he was a pitcher in a jam and I was the coach trying to lighten the mood with bad jokes were memorable – for me. But better by far have been the many more times when my place has been a seat in his audience. I could never have imagined the first time Chris and I saw *Les Miserables* when Max was an infant that one day we'd get to see him play the role of Jean Valjean in a high school production. Or that his encore to that would be the title role in *Jesus Christ Superstar* the following year. The DVD's we purchased of those performances don't even amount to reasonable facsimiles of what I remember about them.

I don't know that we have any footage of him playing baseball, except for a short feature of him and his brother going at it in the front yard. But I am glad that the hole left by his departure for college can be at least partially and occasionally filled by cueing him up on an iPod.

There is much more disappointment between fathers and their children, particularly sons, that is imagined by one party or the other than is real. In the cases of me and mine, I can be sure that I feel none.

My recurring tip to Max is rather generic and Shakespearean: "To thine own self be true." It squares with a quote attributed to Willie Mays: "Maybe I was born to play ball – maybe I truly was."

Max is decidedly not the curricular type and I suspect he is bound to go wandering, a troubadour with a rucksack full of self-belief.

We'll see.

Last year Ben played his final season in the Senior League, top rung on the ladder of good old fashioned Little League. That program is a rotting carcass now left by the AAU and USSSA after they've filled up on the *serious* ballplayers. As a result its kinship to baseball [as the game was meant to be played] is nearly as distant as tee-ball's at the other end of the age range.

Routine pop-ups drop to the ground like something parachuted into a primitive civilization to the astonishment of the local infielders. Fly balls soar across the skies and are regarded as comets or meteors by awestruck outfielders. I've seen teenaged players that haven't even mastered the concept of tagging up on fly balls. This equates to a licensed driver being unaware of the right-turn-on-red exception in the rules of the road.

There's still a certain charm about the traditional Little League culture that only attaches to leagues consisting of neighbors and classmates. Triumphs, no matter how ungainly they appeared on the field of play; no matter how hapless the opponent; are as boasted of the next day at school as would be the achievement of manhood courtesy of a homely but promiscuous girl.

Meanwhile the *serious* ballplayers barnstorm from tournament to tournament like so many packs of over-bred puppies, outfitted to the nines with gear that would have surpassed what big leaguers made do with when I was a little leaguer. Their parents follow, documentarians decked out in quasi-official team apparel, camcorders fully charged and ever at the ready.

How do I know this? Remember, unable to beat them, we were at the fringe of just such an entourage for several of Ben's younger seasons. Actually, ours was a comparatively grounded and no frills outfit, but there were still names on the backs of uniforms where Chico's Bail Bonds used to be and plenty of trophies and medals to compete for. Such hardware has suffered the devaluation that comes with commonness. At our house the trophy most prized is The Horse's Ass. It was designed by the kids' Grandpa Jerry and is awarded to the winner of the spirited, full-contact games of Monopoly he plays with them, usually, but not exclusively, when we are on vacation at a Minnesota lake. They go at it deep into the summer night, ruthlessly seeking to wipe each other out. Hard won bragging rights drown out the call of the loons when The Horse's Ass changes hands, as it regularly does.

Ben was also on the roster of Roosevelt High School's freshman team last summer. Not to say that the school team has become meaningless, but its primacy has been diluted since *serious* ball-players started flocking together on inter-school district elite squads.

After compiling a record of 2-0 in spot duty as a pitcher on Roosevelt's pitching staff he later declared his retirement from organized baseball. He has indicated a desire to continue playing at the levels of Playstation 3 and fantasy leagues and promises to occasionally accompany his father to a real live game, all expenses paid.

I think that both Ben and his brother played long and well enough to gain the extra appreciation for a close play at the plate that can only come from having been personally involved in one. Sliding in just ahead of a strong, accurate throw is one of life's singular joys. Slipping in past curfew unbeknownst to your parents produces a similar, if sneakier, sensation. Similarly, demonstrating the long arm of the house rules to one's children equates, I've learned, to throwing out a runner who dares you to try.

STUBS

When he was 11, Ben was tabbed to pitch the opener for his team against the perennial league favorites at Raccoon Valley. After a scoreless 1st, the opponents' slugger, twice Ben's size, tagged one deep into the parking lot to put his team in front. The next time through the lineup Ben fanned him.

A camera focused on Ben during and after the two at-bats would not distinguish one from the other. I don't know what that reveals about him, but I think it's a toughness he'll be able to call on throughout his life.

If I'd been a broadcaster assigned to his ballgames I might have described him as the impassive lefty or the enigmatic southpaw or the plucky port-sider. He was always sphinx-like in the heat of competition, even when surrounded in the dugout by bawlers. The most demonstrative betrayal of his feelings that I can ever recall was the time when his eyes sprang a slow, silent leak in the car on the way home after he was pinch-hit for in a key spot of a tournament final. Not a word could be coaxed from him. I suspect he remembers that time too.

He is coming soon to the next of life's jumping off points and is still a well-kept secret, even, I think, from himself. I am excited by his prospects for self-discovery.

Like me, his default setting is idle and he has a nose for easier, softer ways. Unlike me, he is quiet and cyber-savvy. In some ways it has been his misfortune to be slotted in the family's pecking order between an older brother whose life found its focus early on and a younger sister to whom naturally accrue the perks of being the only daughter and last of the line.

Many times Ben has stood by unnoticed while his parents accepted compliments of their other son in the aftermath of some sort of performance by the older brother. It would have been easy, I've often thought, for him to nurture resentment toward Max but, to his credit, he seems not to have done that. To the contrary, they seem to be growing closer to one another.

It is Ben that I most recognize myself in amongst our three. Still, we do not communicate well or easily with one another. Perhaps our likenesses account for that. He resists his feelings much of the time. Grins practically have to escape from him, but when they do they are wide, stretching between his ears like a hammock; conversation is a last resort aimed at reducing rather than drawing attentions, at least at home. So might it be with me if I did not write myself down to be understood that way. Around here, Ben expresses most freely with the dogs who serve their purpose as the family's emotional repository very well. We all exchange feelings with others in the pack via the Setter girls - Mitt Gordon and Maple Irish - like they are ATM's for our affections. The life expectancy for dogs is generally thought to be too short by those of us who keep them, but it squares pretty well with the duration of childhood.

I need to know Ben more before he goes.

Emma used to call me Mister Dad in obedience to a playfully given order. I retain some level of influence in her life even though the dynamics between us haven't been the same since she started yelling "banana split!" as I snoozed on the sofa before leaping off the arm and landing on my gut; cushy as a pole vault pit.

She has spent her middle year of middle school going in for repairs. First it was the dermatologist. Then she needed glasses. Next came the dreaded referral to the orthodontist; something uncalled for in the cases of her brothers. As if garden variety acne weren't enough of a blight on her little girl prettiness, she suffered the additional indignity of a small cyst on the bridge of her nose, right between the eyes. Its removal left a minor scar that she feared would draw unwanted attention and curiosity.

Topping it all off she has to shop for clothes that will pass muster with her parents and her contemporaries in a marketplace that dresses our daughters like they were working girls. She has thick, wavy brown hair and nostrils that flare like fish gills when she laughs. Her personality is as irrepressible as the natural beauty that will emerge from the furnace of adolescence like a precious metal ready for forming. She brims with empathy and compassion, traits not worth much in the early teens that must be held like savings bonds until maturity when, finally, their worth reveals. In the meantime she endures the mean time; that stage of life when girls particularly inflict themselves on one another. Their friendships often seem founded on the premise of keeping one's enemies close enough for surveillance.

She is like her oldest brother in several ways, some unavoidably and others that are deliberate on her part. She has always had an older friend or two and is inclined toward the arts. Lankier, so far, than her peers, she has dabbled in basketball and shows promise if not a killer instinct, but she sings more in her room than she shoots in the driveway. Last year her team lost one game to a suburban steamroller by the preposterous score of 51-3. I foresee more clarinet and curtain calls than rebounds and free throws in the coming years.

Once when Emma was barely of school age we were all at Raccoon Valley. It was one of those chaotic evenings when the boys had overlapping games on different diamonds in different sectors of the complex. Chris and I arrived at different times from different places in different cars. By the times the games had run their courses Emma was off playing with a neighbor friend in the vicinity of the girls' softball diamond. I don't remember if we both assumed the other had her or if we both just forgot about her, but after we rendezvoused back at headquarters and started to divvy up the catch from the fast food drive-thru [at our house we call these meals "sack-o-crap"] we were horrified upon realizing that Emma's fries were placed in front of an empty chair!

I bolted back to my car and raced back to the ballpark at movie chase scene speed. When I arrived I found her playing in a sand pile. She was glad to see me but blissfully unaware that she'd been unwittingly and briefly abandoned by the pair of well-intended dupes that merged to make her.

Still, I insist that she is unforgettable through and through.

Measurements

O ne morning soon after Max had begun living beneath another roof I got out of my car and set out to walk the few blocks from my appointed lot to the building where I work now in the engine room of the Des Moines school district.

My job title is staff writer and I am classified, for HR purposes, as a "specialist." I wish I knew what my specialty was. It's a position created by federal stimulus money and I grabbed it hungrily when it was offered to me despite that it was dangled at the end of a string only two years long.

It was drizzling, gently but steadily.

The storm sewers gargled the rain while car tires rolled over the wet streets making the sound of brushed cymbals. The air freshened as the sprinkle continued and the stroll took on the feel of a rinsing. Besides water I began to feel self-pity dripping off of me as I made my way from one mood to the next.

Sadness gave way to a sense of shame that answered the question of who was I to be feeling blue?

Poor me, walking from my car to the job that came my way in the midst of double digit unemployment. Yeah, pity the squeaky old retread with the pretty schoolmarm wife and the three beautiful, healthy kids. One of 'em's gone off to college an eight-hour drive away. Damn, not counting cell phones and computers we're practically incommunicado! With my luck, the kid'll probably make somethin' of himself and never move back home again.

You sign on for a job that, if you're lucky, gets finished - at least in terms of room and board; kind of like being a "specialist" with no particular expertise and a finite contract. There's no reverse gear.

There's no going back from the drop-off at college to the drop-off at kindergarten, except to the extent that you can take yourself there alone by such means as these for an occasional stolen moment or two at a time. I guess I must allow that one man's manuscript is another man's photo album or video library.

There is the irony that this book is nearly finished though the stories that are its subject have scarcely begun and are not ultimately mine to tell.

The life that most preoccupies us - our own - we are so in the midst of that we can no more see it than we can examine our own innards. The ones most observable and captivating are any that we conspire to begin and can recall literally from their outset.

We have come to that point where the days when all five of us are together at even the level of being in the same town are the exception. Did we appreciate them when they were the norm? Yes, when we had time. Usually we were busy living them. From now on there will have to be travel and trouble and worry about weather and arrangement of schedules and payment of expenses just so we can eat at the same table, talk together face to face and fall asleep under the same roof once in a while.

There are benefits when a grown child leaves home. Everyone has more room. Available hot water is spread between fewer morning showers. One less safe landing on the flight deck at the end of each day has to be recorded before the ranking officers may hit their racks. But the best thing of all is the renewed sheen of the group as a whole.

By the time when we couldn't begin and end each day together anymore was upon us we'd lost some appreciation for that simple joy.

When Max came home for his first visit from college, it came back with him.

They Come in Threes

As I leave you our successors are a combined 47 years old. They are all teenagers. Max has nearly finished that phase of the obstacle course and Emma has just entered it. Ben, as is his lot, is smack in its midsection.

They like and support one another because of what they have in common and despite their differences. What a bonus for their mother and father who, for the most part, delight in the myriad ways their children are different than each other. Our feelings for them are a genus within which each variation amounts to a separate species.

It is reasonable to imagine, without taking for granted, that days are in store when they come home to roost bringing nieces and nephews for their siblings and grandchildren for their parents. Won't that be something?

But first must come the perilous days of demon rum; of cars, cannabis and carnality. The once mighty power of "because we said so" has been reduced to a pop gun against the onrushing hordes of peers and pop culture. Probably our most potent weapon is prayer; stealthy and sneakily powerful. But it has been known to work both sides of a conflict and can also be rather methodical. Ultimately the prayer must be that they prevail, not that they be spared the struggle.

Together they haven't been alive as long as I have separately. And yet each of them is wise to the world in ways that I am not and will not be.

They are of the generation that's technologically facile at the expense of shoe-tying; a dying exercise. Their father is as clumsy now with gadgets as I was with brassiere clasps back in the thrilling darkness of my own formative years

We like to think that we can mulch up our past and sprinkle it on our kids' lives like some magic elder dust to help them grow. Well, maybe a little on our best days. But I am glad that ours have each other to teach and learn from. Over the longer haul of their lives sibling reciprocity will be a more enduring resource than fatherly wisdom.

I hope all of the new loves that attach to their lives will be true and lasting after the fashion of the stuff they are made of.

To think there was a time when they were small enough and I was strong enough and we were all young enough at heart for them to ride me together before I'd buck them off and take them on, one against three, in a wrestling match on the living room carpet. It was never clear whose side the dogs were on.

Expressions of affection, in public or private, were unabashed and demonstrative. Besides ear infections, they grow out of these too. There is amazement at the recollection that you could once literally and completely hold your children and their whole lives in your bare hands.

Then abruptly it was no longer okay for me to lean across the front seat and plant a peck on Max before he got out of the car for school. I think he was in first grade.

Ben was restrained at dropoffs and pickups right from the start; whenever the risk was high of him being linked to us. "Don't make me bring those DNA test results onto the playground, mister!" I'd threaten. "Don't make me put on my 'Dad of Ben' nametag. You know you love me. Your secret's out!"

Emma still ends all of her telecommunications with headquarters by reaffirming, "I love you," but even she has become physically reticent away from home ever since that day when she was in 3rd grade; the day when I arrived early before school dismissed to pick her up and her class was still outdoors enjoying their last recess of the day.

We spotted one another. I tooted the horn. She waved. Each of us grinned at the sight of the other. Then I saw her gesturing toward me while talking to a giggling classmate. Later, when she got in the car and I asked about the conversation, Emma explained that she had pointed me out as her father.

"Why was your friend laughing?" I asked.

"She said, 'That's your dad? He looks as old as my grandpa!'"

Last night there were a few moments of fusion when the four of us who still share the same address were seated at the dining room table wolfing a meal together. The phone rang with a tele-marketer's sense of timing, but it was Max.

The call was passed around along with the goulash. There wasn't much time for either. Emma had to get to choir practice and the newly licensed Ben was driving her.

Chris took her turn on the phone like one of the dogs leaning into a good scratch.

Max didn't have any news. He just called because he felt grips loosening. You could hear him not saying that by listening hard between the lines.

He didn't get much longer than the telemarketer would have. But then, only a moment was required for all of us to give and take what we needed.

And then we were re-scattered like dealt cards. Max had to go practice something somewhere. Ben and Emma argued their way out the door. Chris changed and went to the basement to watch TV on the treadmill.

I tinkered a little with this and then invited the dogs to lie down with me on the bed while I took a couple bites out of a biography of Roberto Clemente that I got for five bucks at a bookstore's going out of business sale.

He was nicknamed Momen as a boy because whenever he was called or asked to do something his response was, "momentito, momentito…"

I smiled when I read that and made a note to tell Ben, who takes a lot of flak from us for muttering, "Jus-sec," *every time* he's summoned.

Then I dozed off.

Chris awakened me after her run and a shower. I regained my sense of day and time and let the dogs out for the day's last crack at fertilizing the snowpack. While they prowled our little patch of tundra I munched a couple of oatmeal cookies, courtesy of our neighborly neighbors.

When the dogs came in, Ben and Emma were right on their heels. I closed the garage and locked us all inside the house before plodding back to the bedroom and changing into my nightclothes. Chris had reclaimed her place in our bed from Mitt and Maple. She did her bedtime reading while I nestled myself in the king-sized cocoon.

Ben and Emma were still up and could be heard downstairs masking their true feelings for one another in the guise of mutual contempt.

Max was somewhere in my thoughts, receding like a tide until the next morning.

When the light clicked off I was already on my way back to sleep.

In the living room the wall clock that we gave ourselves for our first anniversary had just chimed nine and all was well.

How dared we, all of this?

Author's Note

After the first draft of this book had been completed and was under review, a few things happened that merit inclusion here.

Ben had to make a firm decision whether to audition for the baseball team or the spring play at school. He went for the stage and landed the part of Dewey Maples in a production of *The Diviners*. It opened the same night as the 2010 home opener for the Iowa Cubs, the perfect coincidence to represent the evolution of my interests since becoming a father. I admired him for trying out and was thrilled by each of his three performances in the role. For the first time since before we had children I missed the local team's home opener.

Meanwhile, Max nearly transferred in the spring of his freshman year at Butler in the wake of some turmoil in his personal life. Chris reprised the midnight ride when she delivered him back to campus after his spring break and during her own with a stopover in Chicago to re-audition at DePaul before continuing on to Indianapolis. By the time they reached there very late on a Monday evening and he was welcomed back to his home away from home by roommates and buddies he'd met just months earlier, he'd come back to his senses and realized he was right where he wanted to be.

Later that week he had a vocal recital that we could only attend in spirit. He sent us a CD recording of it which we listened to some while watching Butler's stirring basketball team lock up the school's first ever berth in *The Final Four* of the NCAA tournament which was held, poetically, in downtown Indianapolis. One of Max's music professors was involved in arrangements for pre-championship game pageantry and he contrived a duty for Max that included free admission to the big game.

On the same day that Butler ultimately lost by a scant two points in the national championship game to mighty Duke [the subservience of a butler to a duke in the pecking order of things made the Bulldogs a decided underdog to the Blue Devils] the Cubs were trounced in their 2010 season opener by the Atlanta Braves. Max spent that day in class and rehearsal for a performance of Brahms' *Requiem*. Ben and Emma [a member of the props crew] were also in rehearsals after school for *The Diviners*.

When Max returned home for the summer he had already planned a baseball barnstorming junket through the Midwest with an old high school chum. He and Sam first met when Max started marching band camp at Roosevelt as a 9th grader. As a trumpeter, he was assigned to a section led by Sam who was two years ahead of Max in school. They became friends by virtue of their shared love of music. By the time Sam graduated and moved on to study composition as a tooting kangaroo at the University of Missouri-Kansas City, Max had returned Sam's influence by bringing him into the fold as a Cub fan. I scrounged up an old baseball card of Carmen Fanzone, a journeyman Cub third baseman from the 70's who had also been accomplished enough as a hornblower to have played the national anthem before games occasionally at Wrigley Field and gave it to Sam as an inexpensive memento of his graduation from high school into the beleaguered and monastic ranks of Cubbism.

Now the two collegians, both aspiring artists, embarked upon an itinerary that would take them to games in Kansas City, Minneapolis and Chicago over the course of a week. Coincidentally, I was going with my friend and neighborhood rival, Gino Redbird, to the game in Chicago between the Cubs and Cardinals on Friday, May 28 that marked the beginning of the Memorial Day weekend and the end of Max and Sam's junket.

We tentatively planned a pregame rendezvous on Waveland Avenue that never happened because of traffic on the expressway and the trains that prevented the arrival in Wrigleyville of Gino and me until just in time to make it to our seats for the National Anthem. By then Max and I had been volleying phone calls all morning and when it became clear that our appointment with one another would have to be canceled I was struck by a profound separation that overrode our presence at the same venue and event. I was not about to resort to standing and waving at one another from across the ballpark while glued to cell phones as is so commonplace nowadays. It would have been a poor substitute. We mourned the Cubs' loss that day from distant sections of the park.

The following Friday tickets went on sale through Ticketmaster for "Max Wellman – Live With His Big Band!" at Hoyt Sherman Place in Des Moines on July 31, 2010. It will be a helluva show and a great night out together for our family. We're buying four of the high-priced seats. One of us won't need a ticket.

Megabus came to Des Moines in the spring, adding a daily route between here and Chicago. Seats reserved early could be had for as little as a buck each way. I couldn't resist and booked three roundtrips for a truly grand total of $24. Then I went in search of tickets for the Cubs' game versus the Pirates on Monday, June 28. In recent years there would have been none available directly through the Cubs for a summer home game with a divisional opponent by the time I went looking. But this edition of the team, despite its status as the national league's highest paid [and most costly to watch - on more levels than just the annually calculated Fan Cost Index], was a study in underachievement and the capacity crowds that now routinely decorate the old ballpark have begun to fray at the edges. I had no trouble ordering three upper deck reserved seats together from the least expensive, as opposed to cheapest, pricing tier.

The bus schedule put us at Union Station in Chicago by late afternoon. From there we hailed a cab, hopping in with an indifferent, sullen hack who ignored my cheerful greeting. The only thing he said before dropping us at the Jackson Street "L" station was *"WHY DONCHA JUST SHUT THE FUCK UP?"* in hollered response to a suggestion offered by a traffic cop who was nearly run over when we whizzed past; that and a mumbled p.s. that was half explanation, half apology about the long day getting on his nerves. I tipped him in the same spirit that shopkeepers pay protection dues to the mob.

There was just enough time to stop at a bunkhouse where we could drop our shared overnight bag and continue on to Wrigley Field, arriving in time for a pregame ceremony that marked the 50th anniversary of "Cub legend" Ron Santo's debut in major league baseball. That event made a much better excuse for all the trouble of the quick back and forth journey than merely going to see the Cubs play baseball, practically against themselves.

Watching Santo stand on two prostheses at the front edge of the pitchers' mound and bounce the ceremonial first pitch up to the plate at a place where he played third base well enough to win five gold gloves during his career was a poignant moment after scrambling to arrive in time.

Our diminished means since the glorious near-miss of 2003 were commensurate to the demise of our team in the standings over that period of time. Not only were we traveling in the steerage of a bus and sitting in the steerage of upper deck reserved, we were bunking in the steerage of a Lincoln Park hostel; a glorified dormitory. I thought it the practical thing to do since we needed only a place to lay our heads for several hours and rinse off the next morning before bussing right back home. We got a private space with a couple of bunk beds and its own bathroom to boot! The place had kind of a Michener/"The Drifters" vibe about it. I may have been the oldest person there and I felt like someone lunging toward loved ones from the dock as they sail out of reach and view. The trip felt almost sudden and was a scaled back economy version in all material ways of the Chicago trips from our shared past. But we did it with feeling.

Ben finally voiced this time what had always seemed true: he doesn't like to ride on the "L." Really, neither do I. So we did as little of that as possible and walked as much as we dared. We shared a meal as good as McDonalds can provide at the one across from the ballpark once we'd finally reached Wrigleyville. While we ate we chuckled at compared notes recalled from earlier visits. Then we jaywalked across Clark Street, entered the stadium and climbed the ramps to our seats. Not only were they in the most affordable section, they were in the very last row of it! That was easily spun into the greater fact that we would have nothing in back of us except the breeze and a great view of the sunset in the middle innings.

We shared more laughs upon the discovery that consecutive seats in the middle of the row were numbered 10 and 112. Only at Wrigley, which for all the charms of its playing grounds, seems in many ways to have been designed by the same befuddled minds that concocted all of the diagonal and maze-like intersections that mark the streets in that part of town. Like the city where it stands, Wrigley Field is much easier to reach than maneuver in.

All around us were people who came only to drink and snap pictures of one another; in particular a large group of young women who seemed devoted to the Cubs inasmuch as they all wore at least one item that pledged their allegiance to the team, but were otherwise oblivious and indifferent as to its fortunes on the field. There is a blissful, chemically induced detachment from the goings-on of the games that seems to be the main attraction of them for more and more folks nowadays. People pose themselves for snapshots like they are sticking their head in plywood cutouts at a carnival to appear as silly caricatures of cowboys or astronauts or, in this case, baseball fans.

Max was determined to track the game on a scorecard despite constant interruptions from his brother and father. I was reminded of his determination to do the same thing when we'd been at the All-Star game in Seattle years ago. I'd warned him then that all-star games are difficult to score because of the steady stream of substitutions that are endemic to them but he didn't listen. Now he was always about a batter behind as he tried to simultaneously hold up his end of the conversation.

He made an off-handed reference to the Toronto Blue Jays' back-to-back World Series crowns in the early 90's. I challenged him, saying they may have won two, but not consecutively. We made a small wager which was almost immediately settled in his favor by a source he tapped into on his I-pod Touch; the contemporary equivalent of calling the library which was how we used to settle such disputes of empirical fact when I was a teenager.

Ben demanded a hot dog within half an hour of downing two double cheeseburgers, a large fry, a large coke and a chocolate sundae across the street. I obliged and we also shared the traditional bag of peanuts. I scored the first triple [three nuts in one shell] of the game and we swapped gulps of a quart-sized soda that became sprinkled with flecks of peanut skins and shells during the couple of innings it took us to down it. But I balked when he later invoked another more spendthrift precedent from other trips to Wrigley Field – he wanted to make the rounds of the souvenir shops in search of a cap he would never have worn after that evening.

The brothers joined forces in lobbying me to go to our favorite Chicago pizza house after the game. I also opposed that idea on the grounds that it would be too late to venture all the way downtown. Fortunately a lady in front of us overheard. After apologizing needlessly for eavesdropping, she informed us that the restaurant in question had a branch office just a few blocks down Sheffield Avenue from the ballpark. After staying until the bitter end of a 2-1 game that tipped in favor of the Pirates [a team that came into the game having lost 17 straight on the road] in the top of the 9th, the three of us went there and shared a stuffed deep-dish pizza like the ones we'd eaten many times in Chicago going back to when they both were little boys.

In the background there was news on the TV about Carlos Zambrano being suspended from the team in the wake of a dug-out tirade aimed at his teammates a couple of days earlier. The rich and enigmatic pitcher who used to scribble autographs for Max and Ben when he was still rising through the minor leagues has become as likely to throw a tantrum as a good ballgame and was now headed for anger management counseling. We head-ed for our dorm room, walking all the way back there, arriving about midnight. Ben was sorry to see that the pool table in the day room was already in use by a couple of young backpackers with European accents. I, his intended opponent, was not.

We bedded down in our spartan quarters which fell quiet right away except for a small air conditioner wheezing at us from the window. I was on one bottom bunk with Ben above me. Max had the other all to himself. While my bunkmate busied himself pen-ciling out the allocations of his soon-to-come first paycheck from his recently landed first job, his brother multi-tasked on an I-pod and a book.

I felt strangely comfortable tucked beneath a thin sheet and a threadbare blanket clutching one biscuit-sized pillow with my head resting on another. Exhausted and untroubled, I fell asleep with the lights still on.

I awakened ahead of my companions the next morning and got showered and dressed before rousing them. We nibbled at the continental breakfast buffet in the hostel commons before heading back to Union Station for the bus ride home.

When we boarded we took three quarters of a seating arrangement in mid-coach that consisted of two pairs of opposing seats. The fourth was filled with our carry-ons. It became clear that there would be no empty seats on the return leg and when a young mother with three small kids in tow came down the aisle in search of four seats together it was Max who readily offered her ours. That meant the three of us would have to scatter with Ben and I ending up near the front and Max clear at the back. I looked back and saw him chatting affably with the random stranger seated next to him and thought how much like his grandfather [who died in 1993 when Max was not quite two] he is; chivalrous and easy with people. Then I leaned across the aisle and playfully punched on Ben, who feigned annoyance that was betrayed by an unstoppable grin he tried to stuff in his pillow. I know that move. He may have learned it from me. Never let 'em see you smile.

Finally, four days later Ben and I drove north together to scout the Minnesota Twins' new ballpark over the Fourth of July weekend. We had great seats in an outdoor venue that was cause for lifting an embargo I'd imposed on the grounds of the team's former grounds; the austere warehouse known as the Metrodome, a godforsaken baseball facility where fielders sometimes lost pop-ups and fly balls against the background of a Teflon roof! The only roofs I noticed here were the carved limestone ones on the dugouts. The grounds were as verdant as Wrigley's and ringed with all of the latest in stadium creature comforts.

Prior to the game a pod of Navy Seals jumped from a plane and steered themselves to an impressive series of landings on the playing field. It was an awe-inspiring display of the raw gallantry of soldiers that utterly transcended the politics of war, brought the capacity crowd to its feet and set the tone for a lively afternoon.

The game itself was highlighted by two homers smote by Jim Thome, the first of which tied him on baseball's all-time HR list with former Twin great Harmon Killebrew [a self-fulfillingly prophetic slugger's name that could never have resulted in a figure skater] and the second of which, number 574 of a career unsmudged by allegation of Incredible Hulk injections, pushed him into sole possession of 10th place in the pantheon of long-ballers. In honor of the occasion Ben gulped two big cans of Killebrew root beer, one of the new palace's featured refreshments.

We drove straight home afterward and as we approached the outskirts of Des Moines at dusk community fireworks displays were breaking out all around us. The orgiastic finale of one practically spotlighted us as we drove almost directly beneath it on Interstate 35.

Ben thought out loud that it was pretty cool. I filed the pleasant thought that it had somehow been as precisely timed as the last scene of a long-running play.

LaVergne, TN USA
19 November 2010
205486LV00002B/3/P